YOU. ARE. LOVED.

Live the Love Song

BY: LISA HEATON

ISBN: 978-1-7320068-5-0

Published by: Faith Forward Press
Mt. Juliet, TN

OTHER TITLES BY LISA:

ACKNOWLEDGMENTS

Amy and Emily, I can't express my love and gratitude enough for all you've both done to keep me on track, keep me believing, and sometimes keep me sane. This has been the hardest-fought battle of my career, but because of you, I was able to see it through to completion.

You are my Aaron and Hur, sisters and co-laborers in the faith who make up for my weakness with your strength.

May God bless you and keep you both. I pray this is just our beginning in ministry together.

You. Are. Loved. by me.

YOU. ARE. LOVED.

From the beginning:

One summer morning, I was about to walk away from my quiet time with God the Father. I specify God the Father since I often address Him according to my need. That morning, I needed the Father's ear. All this time later, I can't remember what was so pressing, just that this girl needed her Dad.

As I stood to walk away, I heard as clearly as I've ever heard Him speak, "You are loved." The words were choppy and specific, more like: You. Are. Loved. I paused mid-stand and then sat back down. With my eyes closed and a grin tugging at my lips, I said back to Him, "You are loved." I sat a while and listened but nothing more happened.

I started to stand again but then stopped. Before I walked away from a word so intimate, I had to ask myself this question: What will my day look like if I live it loved? A few things came to mind, like how I would live out my day with purpose and intention. I was working on a massive revision project at the time and needed focus. I reminded myself that God would be with me. It was, after all, His kingdom work I was accomplishing. I knew I could live out my day trusting that He would provide what I needed.

That's about all I came up with, so I moved on about my day. Many times throughout the day those three words came to mind: You Are. Loved. Each time, the memory made me smile, and a warm feeling washed over me. Different than my many decades before, I now know I'm loved by God the Father and Jesus the Son, my Beloved. Living loved is not new to me anymore. It's not something I take for granted by any means, but after about a decade of living loved, I know what love feels like. It's what I needed all my life. To me, love is the biggest deal. I wallow in it and revel in it and am constantly amazed by it. I now know that I was just as loved during my broken years as I am now, but I had failed to grasp it and pull it into my belief system. It was an elusive ideal that I knew was true, but I hadn't taken hold of it as my personal possession.

Later that night as I was settling in with my husband to watch TV, I was scanning through something on my phone while we waited for our show to begin. I heard music on the TV that caught my attention, so I glanced up. There were no words, but the tune was familiar. When I saw that it was just some commercial, I looked back at my phone, figuring the song was familiar because I had seen the commercial before.

For some reason, I glanced back up at the TV at just the right time and heard, "You are loved." That was it. The letters "ADT" appeared on the screen. It was a home security commercial that was using the Christian song by Stars Go Dim. The tune was familiar to me because I adore that song. I had even used it at conferences where I had spoken – of course, the Jesus Loves Me Conferences.

I was so blown away that I just sat staring at the TV. Then I tried to tell my husband, Kelly, about it. About what an impact it made. Father God had spoken those exact three words to me that morning in a way that stopped me in my tracks. He even made a commercial about it to drive the point home, like bookends at the beginning and end of my day. That was serious planning on His part.

When things like that happen and He begins to weave together chords of revelation through repetition, then I know He's up to something. The next morning, I began to jot down a few notes of how I might use this subject as a possible book or study. Since I was working on that revision project and knew I didn't currently have time to devote real attention to it, I decided to hold off a few weeks until vacation. I figured if God planned on me writing a book, then the fire would fall when the time was right.

I'm not sure that you can call what happened on that vacation fire falling. One event after another hindered me from devoting time to writing until once, when I was at my most frustrated, the commercial came on again. It served as confirmation that I was to write about this topic someday.

That season wasn't His timing, but eventually, other small sparks of thought came together, fire fell, and I got started. Then I stopped again. Then fire fell again. Now I see that each delay has only provided deeper revelation and given me more insight.

One notable thought from my vacation emerged and has carried over into this book. My email devotion contained the following verse. It wasn't in my usual translation, but the timing of it kicked off one of those sparks of revelation.

> *"Yahweh, your God, is in the midst of you, a mighty one who will save. He will rejoice over you with joy. He will calm you in his love. He will rejoice over you with singing."* (Zephaniah 3:17 WEB)

This just happens to be one of my of my favorite verses, one that comes at just the right time as a reminder that God is there, watching and in charge.

I have begun with this long story filled with minute details of how this book came about for this reason: to illustrate and emphasize that God is in our midst, just as Zephaniah says. He is in the small details of your life and my life just as surely as He's in the big ones. That's where people miss God at His most loving, in the minutia of their daily lives.

As further proof of His presence along this journey, a major new component of this project was added well into the process of writing it. This book is divided into two primary sections: Part One contains the foundational concepts that highlight God's love and how knowing you are loved will shift your entire life's perspective. Part Two is made up of individual topics that depict what living loved can or should look like in that particular area.

You. Are. Loved.

Though I understood the connection and how the two parts were irreversibly intertwined and dependent on the other, I had been at a loss as to how to explain it with clarity. I was missing the imagery.

I continued to pray until the answer finally came just the morning before I was to speak on this You. Are. Loved. topic for the first time. It was early morning when I prayed, "Help me explain it. Give me a way to express it." I heard only two words: *a dance*. That was all it took. From there all the pieces fell into place. His love is the music; the lyrics, His Word. Your faith walk is the dance you live out in relationship with Jesus.

That brings me back to Zephaniah 3:17, and how this phrase sings a new melody: *"He will rejoice over you with singing."* This life He has given us is His love song sung over us. I now offer this book as a verse in my love song of praise back to Him. I pray you draw closer to the lover of your soul so that you may hear the music of His love playing louder every day.

May your heart catch on fire so that you sing a love song in return with the way you live loved.

My hope is to show you what I've been shown, to tell you what I've been told, and to give you what I've been given. Recently, I acknowledged in prayer that I have no right to be writing this book. Jesus reminded me: Who better to write about the dance than one who's lived it?

I'm not a pastor, minister, or theologian. I am, however, a woman who has done it wrong most of my life. More importantly, I am a woman who has learned to dance to the melody of His love. I've been transformed in ways that I can hardly believe. Oh, I'm still a mess in many areas, but I've been healed by the love and grace of God. Nothing matters more to me than sharing God's love. I know of no better way to express the work the Holy Spirit has done in me other than through examples from my own journey. I am living the love song; come dance and sing along with me.

Grace and Peace,
Lisa

BEFORE WE BEGIN

I can't, in good conscience, begin this book without asking this question: Do you belong to God the Father through Jesus the Son? You can't count on childhood baptism or family connections for the answer. There has to be a moment in your life when you admit you are a sinner and accept what Jesus did on the cross to save you from a life apart from Him. Have you done that?

You are loved by God the Creator before accepting Jesus, but you aren't yet a child of God the Father until you experience salvation through the cross.

Without the Spirit of God indwelling your spirit, something that happens when you invite Jesus to be your Savior, you can't experience the life of living loved that I am about to describe. A sense of walking in the cool of the day, as we will consider next, isn' possible for the person who isn't walking with God.

Maybe your walk of faith has been tentative. Maybe you' new to the faith and can't yet say a resounding yes simply becau this terminology is so new to you. In any case, I invite you to re on. I will tell you much about Jesus and God the Father and h deeply You. Are. Loved. If you don't know Him, then allow me introduce you to Him. Living loved is knowing Jesus.

If you stumbled upon this book and have questions on ho invite Jesus into your life, find a believing friend or turn to the C News page in the back of this book. I invite you to know the I know.

PART ONE

IN THE COOL OF THE DAY

Recently, during my quiet time, a phrase came to mind about walking with God: in the cool of the day. It was as if He was reminding me that walking with Him should feel like that, restful. I love that this book begins with the beginning. I'm not strategic enough to have planned that on my own.

"And they heard the sound of the LORD God walking in the garden in the cool of the day, and Adam and his wife hid themselves from the presence of the LORD God among the trees of the garden." (Genesis 3:8)

Usually when this verse is quoted, the focus is on the sin aspect, but that's not where I want to draw your attention. I want to point out that God's original design for man (and woman) was for us to walk with Him in the cool of the day. That's what living loved should look like. To walk with the Lord in the cool of the day should be a life of peace and acceptance and purpose.

Punishment for the original sin included mankind being expelled from the Garden of Eden, preventing humans from walking with God physically as Adam and Eve did. In a spiritual sense, that barrier was removed with the rending of the veil when Jesus was on the cross. We now have full access to walk with God the Father and Jesus the Son through the Holy Spirit. We are invited to that walk every day of our lives.

When God questioned him regarding his sin, Adam's response was:

*"Then the man said, 'The woman whom You gave to be
with me, she gave me of the tree, and I ate.' "*
(Genesis 3:12)

Never underestimate the tremendous sway you have over your husband, home, and family. Take great care how you wield your power. Yes, Adam should have been the leader of his home and said no to the temptation, but Eve had an influence over her husband that altered the course of human history.

Consider this: If you know you are loved and live your life as if you are, there is a much better chance your family will follow suit. Our children tend to model our behavior. Our husbands take cues from us as well. This topic is critical for your life; it's vital that you live loved in front of the ones you love. They will only want what you have if what you have is inviting.

The latter part of the verse says:

"The woman said, 'The serpent deceived me, and I ate.' "
(Genesis 3:13)

I'm not sure why this verse has never impacted me in the past the way it has recently, but for whatever reason it's now stuck in my head, often ringing out in my own circumstances. I've been given a fresh revelation, a new way to view this verse:

The serpent is still deceiving, and we are still eating.

The enemy feeds us lies, and we eat. We eat until we're so full of doubt that we can hardly believe God is good. The enemy convinces us that what we are experiencing in our Christian walk is all there is, that our mediocre lives are what we are stuck with. We have no reason to believe there's more since we've never experienced more.

I'm here to tell you that's not true. You and I are designed to walk in an intimate relationship with God where we hear His clear leading, a walk where we feel loved and live our lives based on His truth. The Church as a whole isn't walking with God in the cool of the day. Most are hiding among the trees after eating what the serpent has fed them.

The list of lies we believe is a mile long: I am worthless, pointless, and aimless. I'm unlovable. There is no hope. I hold on to yesterday as if I might change it and fear tomorrow as if worry might affect the outcome. I'm too fat, too thin, too short, too tall. I'm not pretty enough or smart enough or capable enough. I have nothing to contribute. God could never love me.

The most detrimental deception we swallow is doubting God's love and faithfulness, which leads us to wonder if God really has our best interest at heart. Will He fail me? Why didn't He heal? Why did He allow?

There is something about settling the love issue that, with time, unravels all the other doubts. I say with time because trusting in His love doesn't happen overnight.

From my own experience, the most effective lie the enemy has ever fed me was to doubt God's love for me. If I doubt that, nothing else works: not trust or surrender or accomplishing what I was created to do. All it takes for the enemy to defeat and cripple us is to cause us to doubt the completeness of God's love.

Let's consider what it might look like to walk in the cool of the day with Jesus. We need inspiration, a reason to pursue this topic of grasping God's love and living loved. We all need a finish line in sight to urge us on.

If you walk in the cool of the day with Jesus, you:

-    Know that He is enough
-    Hear from God
-    Keep reading the Love Letter
-    Walk in the moment
-    Reflect who He is to others

This is far from a comprehensive list, but it's enough to give you an idea of what you can look forward to.

One of the things I love about God is how He can tailor His work in my life to me and at the same time be the God you need. He knows us and meets us individually. Consider this from the Psalms:

"He fashions their hearts individually; He considers all their works." (Psalm 33:15)

In my own walk, the cool of the day means: I feel no pressure of impending things. Whatever His call and plan, I know He will carry it out and empower me to do my part. The weight of the world is on His shoulders, not mine. I am at rest from worry. He calms my fears. Past moments of His faithfulness remind me He will come through, just as He always has.

I feel exhilaration while with Him, no matter the gloom and doom that awaits me in the world. I find time flies, and I have to tear myself away from Him. It hasn't always been like that. There were times in my life when I was kind of phoning it in, making time to read a little and pray a little. Now, I get so absorbed in the moment that I find myself running late for what's next in my day. That's a good thing. I can live with that.

I grow along the walk. He accepts me as I am but refuses to leave me that way. Every season brings to light new places for growth and allows for His continued work in making me more like Him.

The cool of the day isn't just a quiet time experience, something you only recognize while reading your Bible or spending time in prayer. It's a life experience. Jesus wants to hang out with you. He wants you to live out this life knowing love so penetrating that your daily life reflects Love.

"Come to Me, all you who labor and are heavy laden, and I will give you rest. Take my yoke upon you and learn from Me, for I am gentle and lowly in heart, and you will find rest for your souls. For My yoke is easy and My burden is light." (Matthew 11:28-30)

The cool of the day feels like that, rest for your soul. If you don't know love so restful, prepare for a journey where you will come to know His love with such certainty that you will live each day of your life loved.

BE LOVED

It stands to reason that in order to live loved you must be loved. You are. That's a given. Your state of being is loved. Not only are you loved, you will always be loved, and nothing can take God's love away from you. Paul expresses God's steadfast love in this way:

"For I am persuaded that neither death nor life, nor angels nor principalities nor powers, nor things present nor things to come, nor height nor depth, nor any other created thing, shall be able to separate us from the love of God which is in Christ Jesus our Lord."
(Romans 8:38-39)

You. Are. Loved. Thing is, most of us either don't feel loved or we underestimate the love God has for us, which drives our actions. It's merely a clinical practice to know in your head that God loves you. Knowing it in your heart and experiencing it daily is what actually transforms you. Love is the key to every locked door in your soul. It's a divine thing to know God's love, a happening only the Holy Spirit can ensure.

I pray Ephesians 3:17-19 over you now, that Christ may dwell in your heart, that you would be rooted and grounded in love and comprehend what is the width and length and depth and height of it – to know the love of Christ which passes knowledge.

Since feelings lie, I am reluctant to use the word *feel* when I say you must feel loved. What I actually mean is that it must become real to you, feel as in experience and receive and absorb and believe.

To know that I am loved shapes who I am and what I do and how I live out my kingdom purpose. It will for you, too. You look different when you are loved. You act different when you are loved. You are different when you are loved well by the One who created you to desire His love above any other.

The God who is in the midst of us is not just in the midst of the collective us. He is in the midst of us as individuals. He is dwelling in us personally, loving us in the exact way we each need to be loved. He knows what you need long before you do.

To feel loved by God isn't usually an overnight process, something that necessarily happens along with salvation. It didn't happen that way for me, and many people I know experience the same thing. The sense of being loved unconditionally actually came after watching Him love me unconditionally through my worst failures. His faithful love was evident when He never gave up on me, no matter how many times I turned from him. Devoted love was there day after day as I healed after a destructive season while walking apart from God. Even when I pushed Him away, He took another step closer. His perseverance and patience in waiting for me to come around eventually unraveled me.

I returned to Him covered in the mire of this world. The fact that I had turned my back on God at all forced me to take an honest look at my heart when compared to the verse: *"Love the Lord your God with all your heart, soul, and mind"* (Matthew 22:37).

I didn't love Him with my all or even with my most. I wanted to. Because of my history of a desperate need for human love, my perspective was skewed, and I found it hard to believe that fulfilling love was possible with Jesus. My approach was, as I said before, clinical. It was a mental assent that I gave to loving God. I loved Him as in I revered Him. I saw Him as holy. I loved Him as much as my heart was able to at the time. But deep down, I didn't love Him with all my heart, soul, or mind.

That eye-opening revelation, the fact that my lack of love for Him was responsible for my walking away from him, started me on a journey. I was determined to love Him. I sat with Him and told

Him that He was to be my pursuit. I chased after Him in every way I knew how. I began each day reading my Bible, even when it didn't give me any new insight. I listened to sermons, like, *really* listened. I worked to apply what I was learning to my life.

This new pursuit of mine was just like my old way of doing things before walking with God. I believed I could actually do it on my own as if it were up to me. I was pretty well versed in my Bible at the time but never considered the passage that says we love because God first loves us (1 John 4:19). Come to find out, I didn't need to chase what had been there all along: His love.

I love the title of this chapter, *Be Loved*, since those two words eventually converged and gave me my new name. It was actually through a work of fiction where the main character called his wife Beloved that the word began to resonate with me. I found it followed me long after the story ended. It banged like a drum in my head and was all I could hear, no matter what was going on around me. I would be in the middle of a conversation or watching TV and hear, "Beloved, Beloved, Beloved." Until then, I had experienced very few moments where I was certain I was hearing the voice of God.

From that point on, the word was everywhere: in sermons, devotions I was reading, and my daily Bible reading. Maybe my awareness was simply heightened, but the word chased me relentlessly until finally I succumbed to the truth of it. I was God's loved one, His Beloved. I went from being a lifelong unloved woman to a woman loved, knowing I was loved, and experiencing His love. Other than salvation, nothing has impacted my life in any greater way than discovering I was loved by Jesus. All my years of searching, all my years of disappointing, wounding human love led me to true love, to Jesus. No matter what happens in this tragic world I live in, I know one thing: I. Am. Loved.

Out of the overflow of His love for me, I was able to finally love Him in return. I love Him with all my heart and soul and mind. I don't always do a good job of it, but I love Him. He gives me grace when I get it wrong and teaches me lovingly. I love Him better now than I did ten years ago. I have no doubt that I'll love Him better ten years from now.

At the time I began that journey, I assumed everyone already felt loved by God. I assumed the believers around me loved Him with their all. When in Sunday school or women's studies, I was certain I was the only one who hadn't "gotten it" all that time. Of course, I was too embarrassed to share my story at first. I never asked anyone how someone as broken as me could love and be loved by a Holy God. Following my usual pattern, I did what I had always done and tried to figure it out by myself.

Now, all these years later, I know others are feeling what I felt – as if something is missing. They are faking it through this thing called a faith walk just like I did. So many settle for a cup when an ocean of soul-quenching love is offered.

Beloved of the Lord, take hold of His love and draw it so deep into your longing soul that you refer to yourself as the disciple whom Jesus loves – present tense. Hear it echo in your heart and soul and mind. That's what takes you captive, His intimate Love.

This topic of being loved strikes you one of two ways: You shout, "Yes! This is what I've found, and the world needs to know it." Or you whisper, "That's exactly what I need, to be loved as I am."

Either way, before you move on take some time to consider the following questions with great intention. Take as much time as you need. Spend time with God in prayer. Don't just ask yourself these questions. Ask God His truth. If you struggle with believing you are loved, cry out, "Help me overcome my unbelief!" You can believe God's priority is for you to know His love with certainty.

LOOK WITHIN:

Do you feel so loved that it shapes your day-to-day life, or does God's love for you seem to be more of a mental exercise than a sense of heart experience?

_____

Is the love you have for Him intimate and personal?

_____

What are you willing to invest in the journey to come: time, attention, a willing heart?

_____

_____

If you are already walking out this love journey with Jesus, hallelujah! Pray for others who are reading this, that they will know His penetrating love by experience. The topics we cover in Part Two will still challenge you to view each day as an opportunity to live your life and dance the dance with such purpose that others see Love through you. In a world that's turning up the heat, we need a fresh reminder of what it feels like to walk with the Lord in the cool of the day.

If you don't currently experience His life-altering, completing love, then how do you get to that place? The first step is in getting to know the many facets and the radiant glory of your Walking Companion.

YOUR WALKING COMPANION

In the physical realm, you can't love or receive love from someone you don't know. You can admire, respect, and even follow the teachings of a person, but sincere love isn't achieved without intimate knowledge. It's the same with loving God.

In the early years of my faith walk, I knew the Sunday Jesus, the one others knew and told me about. I believed in a faraway God the Father. I lived my daily life neglecting the companionship of the Holy Spirit. I sought out others to help solve life's most difficult issues because I didn't believe the Triune God would actually answer my questions. I joined women's Bible studies where I filled in every blank and gained useful knowledge, but I still didn't know God on a personal level.

I spent years doing the right things. On the outside I seemed to have my life in order. I stopped doing the things church people frowned upon, began walking and talking like church people, and even tried to dress the part. However, untended-to business was still lurking beneath my surface. All my adult life I had shoved unhealed trauma into the deepest recesses of my soul.

When the typical Christian life – do-ing the dos and don't-ing the don'ts – didn't work for me, I bailed. Why wouldn't I? I had spent thirty years getting my needs met by the world. Why not go back to what was comfortable? Like a thorn working its way out of flesh, those things from my past reemerged and nearly destroyed me. I was a found person living lost.

What I discovered during my brief time away from God was that old habits no longer had the power to ease my tangled mind. If anything, my worldly ways left me feeling emptier. I was miserable.

Once I realized that being away from Him was even worse than faking my way through church life, I came to my senses. I was exhausted from running and weakened in a way I've rarely been in my life. My spirit was in constant turmoil, so I limped my way back home just like the prodigal son.

During that time, my husband and I were working on an outdoor project that required a large amount of dirt to be brought in to backfill our yard. The dirt was dark and rich and promised to grow healthy grass. I was told it was dirt from a pig farm, well fertilized. We did what we were supposed to do and sowed good seed. We watered, and soon tender grass was shooting up all over. Then they came – weeds like I've never seen before. Overnight tall, ugly, red-thorned weeds had sprouted up and were looming over the new grass. They were everywhere I looked.

In frustration, I began to snap off the weeds and toss them aside. I heard a voice that day say, "If you snap them off, they will only grow back. You have to dig up the root."

The voice was God. I'm not sure how I knew since there was no reason I would recognize His voice at that stage of my life, but I was certain. I went to get a weeding tool and began to pry up root after root. It wasn't long before I looked out over that field of wicked weeds and said, "But there are so many." The voice came again, "Just pull one at a time."

Consider this aspect of the prodigal son's story: Yes, he came home, but what was his life like after his return? I would suppose he could hardly look his dad in the eye. You know he had a strained relationship with his embittered brother. The prodigal lived with guilt and remorse, and he wore the stench of the world on him for a season after his return. You can't walk away from your spiritual home and not rack up debt and consequences that must be lived with.

That pig dirt was symbolic of my time in the world and how I brought the stench of it back home with me. I was not only broken, I was damaged in ways that took the Lord Jesus years to mend. Just to mention a few things: I came back to Him in the middle of a full-blown eating disorder, dependent on alcohol, and filled with shame over my lost-like behavior. I had hurt people I loved, and I was hurting myself. I needed restoration. I needed Jesus.

The Gardener and I worked tireless hours in my garden. The physical weeds were tackled easily. My spiritual weeds, however, were dealt with over the course of many years. Just as He had instructed me to do that day when I was snapping off weeds, He began to dig deep down to the root of the weeds in my heart and mind. One by one He pulled them with a gentle hand.

I wish I could say I'm completely well. Are any of us ever complete here in this life? It's been a long process, but I now know sustained joy and peace, and I love Jesus with true abandon. I'm a different woman than that poor girl who came hobbling home to a Father she didn't even know.

No matter your history, there is healing with God the Father and Jesus the Son through the Holy Spirit who indwells you. No matter how far away God seems to you, I give you my word that an intimate and personal Jesus is waiting to reveal Himself to you. God your Father wants to extend His arms to you and share who He is and how infinitely He loves you. You have to decide to step in closer so that you can see all He wants to show you.

You may not resemble the prodigal son. You may be the big brother who got it right by staying home in the first place, but if your daily life isn't rocked by the love of a tender Father and the beckoning call of the Son, then you still have work to do. You must lean in and get to know the lover of your soul. The Apostle Paul prayed,

> *"...that the God of our Lord Jesus Christ, the Father*
> *of glory, may give to you the spirit of wisdom and*
> *revelation in the knowledge of Him."* (Ephesians 1:17)

In hindsight, I've discovered this truth: There are infinite facets of who God is and who He is willing to be to each of us. What do you need? Do you need a Father's touch? Do you need the companionship of a Friend or the guidance of a Counselor? Only you know the answer to that question. What I hope to give you in the section to come is a jumping off point so that you will run to the God of your need. The way to get to know Him is to expose your weakness and need and then allow Him to invade your situation and be who He already is.

In no way do I want to make this seem as if God is somehow your go-to genie, here to meet your needs and give you a happy life. It's the exact opposite of that. He wants you to see that all your need is wrapped up in Him. He is your life (Colossians 3:4). Until you come to the obvious conclusion that Jesus is all and everything you need, you will continue to live your life as if there might be more out there than your life hidden in Christ. Without a hidden walk with Jesus, you are openly exposed to the dangers and influences of the outward world.

Along with each attribute of God I've described in the following pages, I've provided Scripture references to substantiate my claim that God is the God of all your needs. Don't blow through these without thoughtful consideration. If something resonates with you, look up the verse and make note of it. You may need something to lean on. What better to hold you up than the mighty Word of God?

FACETS OF WHO GOD IS:

Approach God as My Father
(Romans 8:14-16)

- I. Am. Loved. by an infallible Father who has no variation or shadow (James 1:17), a parent always concerned with my well-being. He watches over me while I sleep and while I go about the business of my day. He has compassion on me and remembers my frailty (Psalm 103:13-14).

- He wants to lead me and guide me as any good father would and says, "This is the way, walk in it" (Isaiah 30:21). The unseen Father has made Himself known by sending Jesus the Son (John 1:18).

- When I feel vulnerable and the world seems overwhelming, He is my mighty Dad, a Father to the fatherless (Psalm 68:5) who can take on any foe. He is my protector.

- When I feel lost and far from home, He reminds me that He is waiting for me with open arms (Luke 15:20).

- His Father's heart is always for me – even when I'm a not-so-well-behaved child. He receives and disciplines me because I am His (Hebrews 12:5-6).

- He is my Dad whom I can ask for anything, one who will only give me what's best (Luke 11:9-13).

- God is a Father who will bring me home to be with Him someday (John 14:2, 17:24).

Walk with Jesus My Beloved
(Matthew 12:18-21)

- This Jesus died for my rescue (Galatians 1:4). When I long for romantic love, I know there is no more romantic gesture or happily ever after than when the Hero rides in to redeem me, His beloved (Isaiah 43:1-4). He is my ultimate love story.

- When I am lonely, He is the Lover of my soul and calls me Beloved (Romans 9:25).

- Neither shame nor condemnation has power over me, the one whom Jesus has made clean (Isaiah 54:4-5, Romans 8:1). No matter my history, he has made me white as snow through His sacrifice (1 John 1:7).

- I am accepted in the Beloved (Ephesians 1:6-8). When I feel rejected by this world or by individuals and relationships, Jesus accepts me as I am. He also loves me too much to allow me to stay as I am. He grows and stretches me and removes what is blemished within my human heart. I am a new creation in Christ (2 Corinthians 5:17).

- He listens when no one else will. I can go boldly before the throne (Hebrews 4:16). He cares for me when no one else does (1 Peter 5:7). He is for me and not against me (Romans 8:31). He loves me when others refuse to and willingly died for me while I was still a sinner (Romans 5:8).

- His embrace is enough even when the world tells me that what I need is human love (2 Peter 1:2-4). Human love fails. The God who is Love never fails me (1 Corinthians 13:8).

Fall Before Jesus the King
(John 12:15)

- At the appointed time I will see Jesus appearing as King of Kings and Lord of Lords (1 Timothy 6:15-16).

- Jesus as King will overcome those who wage war against the Lamb. I will be with Him, called chosen and faithful (Revelation 17:14).

- My position is that of a servant (Romans 6:22), a soldier (2 Timothy 2:3-4), and a messenger on His behalf (2 Corinthians 5:20). He has a plan for me and will accomplish great things through me as one submitted to His authority (Ephesians 2:10).

- His power goes before me in battle. The battle is His – not mine – to win. I will stand firm on the battleground (2 Chronicles 20:17).

Meet With the Wonderful Counselor
(Isaiah 9:6)

- I will abide with You forever – the Spirit of Truth (John 14:16-17).

- I know You will guide me with Your counsel (Psalm 73:24).

- The Helper, whom the Father has sent, will teach me all things and bring the Word to my remembrance (John 14:26).

Pursue the Prince of Peace:
(Isaiah 9:6)

-   When the wind threatens, waves roar, and the world clamors, Jesus says, "Peace be still" (Mark 4:39).

-   He is my hiding place, refuge, and shelter (Psalm 32:7, Psalm 61:3).

-   I can cast all my cares upon Jesus because He cares for me (1 Peter 5:7).

-   The Lord gives me strength and blesses me with peace (Psalm 29:11).

Seek the Great Physician
(1 Peter 2:24)

-   Healing is His nature. No matter my ailment, He is the Cure (Matthew 8:1-17). He created my body and knows its every working part (Psalm 139:13-16).

-   Healing may come now. Healing may come tomorrow. Healing may be found only in the eternal. When He doesn't heal here, He heals in heaven (2 Corinthians 5:1-2).

-   For those who become His, he has already healed the greatest sickness known to man – sin (Isaiah 53:5).

The list above isn't exhaustive by any means, but I hope it will trigger your own thoughts as you answer the questions that follow.

Of the men
Father, Belo
below.

Write out y
the Son. Ju
ahead watcl

When you
that meets
heart for ai
Watch for
intimate re

LOOK WIT[

Do you feel yo[
only know the [

———————

Is God as your [
noticeably in y[

———————

Do you believe[

———————

Have you kno[
prodigal, in a [
return:

———————

———————

———————

Have you kno[
through issue[
below.

———————

———————

———————

Have you exp[
examples of h[

———————

INTIMATE RELATIONSHIP

Upon my return to God, I began to get to know and speak almost exclusively to Jesus. It wasn't intentional on my part, but at the time God the Father was still a faraway concept to me. What I needed in that season was the ear of the Wonderful Counselor. My heart needed the Great Physician in order to even beat again.

All these years later, I still have countless needs. So when I walk with God in the cool of the day, the God who walks with me is exactly who I need at that moment. I began this book by telling you I was meeting with God the Father the morning I was given the You. Are. Loved. message. Walking with God based on my specific need has been one of the most beneficial and real aspects of my overall walk with the Triune God. I run to God based on my desperate need of the moment.

At times, when working on this book, no matter how much progress I make, I feel ill qualified, and rightly so. I can't tell you how many times I've just sat with Jesus and shook my head, saying, "I can't do this. It's too big for me." In this instance I sit with Jesus as my King. I am a servant of His kingdom. This is His call on my life in this season.

It never fails that something comes along to remind me it's His power, not my own, that propels this book forward. One morning I read these red-letter words:

"The words that I speak to you I do not speak on My own authority, but the Father who dwells in Me does the works." (John 14:10)

I underlined that verse and even copied it over into my journal as a reminder that it's His resurrection power that dwells within me and will do the work through me. I'm not able. This is too big. But He is able and bigger than any overwhelming task.

That verse was encouraging and powerful, but the truth is I still felt just as overwhelmed. Then I received this text from my young-adult son:

> *Walked by your bible study stuff sitting in the kitchen last night and saw the live loved binder... i remembered you talking about how you don't feel qualified to write the nonfiction stuff that you are writing and a quote came to mind about it.*
>
> *God doesn't call the qualified; He qualifies the called. You got this.*

God was in my midst that morning. Just when I needed it, He gave me the encouragement to keep moving forward no matter my doubt. I'm telling you: God is in your midst just like He is in mine. I hope that by showing you examples of the little and big ways He showed up in my life, confirming His faithful love, you will see He does the same for you. You have to be on the lookout. That verse at the right time was no coincidence. For my son to take the time to send that text was at God's urging. God is in my midst. God is in your midst. Keep your eyes open, and you will see Him.

When the God of all the universe steps into the small places of my daily life, I am amazed. How can that do anything other than prove He's a loving Father and Friend who wants to be a part of my life?

One of the foundational truths you must stand on is God's love for you as a Father. The other is Jesus' love for you. I find their love for me differs, yet is intensely the same. Though I need to be loved on many different levels, the Triune God's capacity for love far exceeds my need.

As many broken women as I have known over the years, I rank right up there with them as one of the biggest messes I've encountered. On the outside for most of my adult life, if you would have met me, you would have thought I was fairly pulled together. That was mere deception on my part. Because I was the victim of sexual abuse as a little girl, I learned early on to be someone else, anyone else but the mass collection of insecurities that raged within me. I was an empty façade, with an underscore on the word empty.

And on top of that, my parents divorced when I was only five, so not having a father in the home chipped away at any foundation of security that I might have had as a little girl. I have a good relationship with my father, and I never doubt his love for me, but back then I felt anything but loved. I'm not even sure I felt abandoned since I don't think I saw it in those terms. Instead, he was just gone from my home, nonexistent in my daily life.

I am tempted to share all the dreadful decisions I've made in life, all the wrong choices that labeled me chief among sinners. That isn't what this book is about. You know what it looks like to try and get your needs met by the world. No matter if it's your own daddy issues you are trying to work through or if your perspective of love is skewed by abuse or abandonment, there is only one thing that matters: God is your Father if you have become His through faith in His Son, Jesus.

Your history doesn't matter. Your family tree doesn't matter. Your past choices don't matter. (Other than you are likely living out consequences of them.) What matters is that you must find a way to God the Father and to know the love He has for you. When I say find a way, that may be misleading since He has never left you. He's right there. Your hindrance may be your own mistrust and false notions of what a real Father looks like.

I personally am still working through this. I drew near to Jesus and developed an intimate relationship with Him long before I could approach God as Father with any comfort. I would sit with Jesus and run off at the mouth for hours at a time, but when it came to Father God, I was shy and timid in my conversations. All the years of this journey, in my mind I have sensed Jesus next to me always. Until recently, God the Father seemed farther away, like I had to travel to get to where He was just so I could pray to Him. I don't experience that distance at all now. Just as Jesus is with me always, I feel the presence of God the Father in my daily life as well. This new relationship with God as my trusted Father has taken years to develop and has required me to believe His Word even when my heart was too wounded to relate to Him as my Father.

Here is what opened my eyes to the difference. One day while in my quiet time, something came to mind. When I was a little girl, if I was at the store with my mom and near the check out, I would start begging for candy or whatever grabbed my attention. I didn't hesitate to ask. If I was visiting my dad and at a store with him, however, I wouldn't ask him for anything. I didn't feel comfortable enough with him to ask since I wasn't actually doing life with him. If he offered, I'm sure I accepted, but I couldn't bring myself to ask my dad for anything I wanted or needed. God brought that memory to mind to show me that I did the same with Him. I would share my deepest needs and wants with Jesus but not with God the Father.

Besides what we covered in our earlier list of the facets of God, Scripture describes Him as having many different roles in our life. Anything you need Him to be He already is. You have no need, spiritual, emotional, or physical that He can't meet.

For some, you may more easily relate to God as Father and struggle with an intimate relationship with Jesus the Son. What many believe, but would never admit, is that to them, Jesus isn't enough. They think, "Jesus is fine to get me to heaven, but He can't actually make me feel less lonely when I'm all alone here on earth, right?" That's the wrong thinking that kept me such a mess for many years, even after I had decided to sincerely walk out my life with God. Deep down, I didn't think He was enough. The serpent deceived, and I ate.

My old need for romantic love was so great that it took the love story of all time to eventually capture my longing heart and break its power over me. Out of my skewed perspective of love and sex, my history had been riddled with one failed attempt after another to fill the emptiness within me through relationships with men. Never once had that worked. When finally desperate enough, I focused on Jesus as my Beloved, and His faithful love ended my relentless pursuit.

What finally opened my eyes? There was a song on Christian radio, "By Your Side," by Tenth Avenue North. Sung from the perspective of Jesus, these were the lines that changed everything: "Why are you looking for love? Why are you still searching as if I'm not enough?"

That was it; those two lines of a song exposed my heart. I was still searching for human love to fill and complete me. I had to sit with Jesus one morning and admit, "You're not enough." I was wise enough to add, "But I want You to be." From there we set off on a journey where Jesus genuinely became enough. He has become my first love, the One I put above all else in my life. All that I do is for Him. Whether it is countless hours banging on a keyboard trying to share my experiences with other women so that they might see Him for who He really is, or searching out the Scriptures, or praying or journaling. It's all for Him. Because the word *in* implies being contained within something or submerged, I can say that I have fallen in love with Jesus. He is who I am now; He in me and I in Him.

Little did I know, all that time I was only willing to meet with Jesus I was missing out on something spectacular: My real Dad. When the grocery store memory came to mind and its implications began to rattle around in my head, I had to sit with God the Father and admit to Him, "I don't really see you as my Father, my Dad who can be trusted. That's why I don't come to You and ask for anything. That's why I hardly talk to You at all."

Conversely, those of you who have close relationships with your earthly dad may struggle as much. If you depend on your dad and his advice here in this life, your soul won't likely long for your Heavenly Dad. You would be wise to look inward, examine your heart, and

You. Are. Loved.

take that to God if you find you lean more on your biological father and less on your adopted Father.

As you get to know God through His Word, the one common theme throughout Scripture is God's love for His children. It is seen throughout the Old Testament and carries over into the New Testament. He pursues us, woos us, and is jealous for us.

"The Lord has appeared of old to me, saying: 'Yes, I have loved you with an everlasting love; therefore with lovingkindness I have drawn you.' " (Jeremiah 31:3)

He loves us with an everlasting love. His love can't be compared to that of the human experience. It is in looking through the lens of human eyes that we underestimate His love for us. While He often uses father/child and husband/wife relationships in Scripture as a basis of comparison of His love for us – something most of us can identify with – we still can never seem to grasp how wide and long and high and deep is the love of Christ (Ephesians 3:18).

We must, at all costs, grasp and take hold of such life-altering love. Love was the game-changer for me. Little things He did for me, little things He has shown me, those signs of affection from Him crept into my heart, softening it toward Him, causing me to dare to believe that such love could actually exist. I can hardly remember the time specifically when the floodgates actually opened and my heart was filled. I remember it seemed sudden, like I went from a woman who desperately needed love to a loved woman. I felt complete in a way I had never known before. Until you have spiritual eyes opened to see God's love for you in action and in your daily life, rely on the Truth of Scripture. God is Love: You. Are. Loved.

Paul prays for us to:

"... know the love of Christ which passes knowledge; that you may be filled with all the fullness of God."
(Ephesians 3:19)

We can be certain of this: His love for each of us is so vast and beyond human perception that, once we even catch a glimpse of it, there comes with it an immense filling of what is said to be the fullness of God. That is when we finally feel complete. That empty place you've always known is a place only God's love can fill.

Contrary to what your deceptive heart tries to convince you of, what you have always wanted and needed can only be found in the Person of Jesus Christ, in intimate relationship with Him and with God the Father in the day-to-day living out of your life. As early as childhood we become convinced that our deepest need for love and worth can be found within the bounds of a human relationship, specifically with the opposite sex. We have accepted the world's view that ultimate love is human love. Not so! Ultimate, completing, fulfilling, and unconditional love can only be found in God the Father and Jesus the Son.

It's time to expose your own heart and determine if an intimate relationship with Jesus is enough for you or if you're still searching as if He's not enough.

LOOK WITHIN:

What is your view of God as your Father? Does it feel like a father/ daughter relationship? Can you call yourself a Daddy's girl?

_____

_____

In what ways have you experienced God's love in your normal, everyday life? Do you sense Him in your midst?

_____

_____

How has God pursued you? What evidence have you seen?

_____

_____

Do you relate more to God the Father or to Jesus the Son? Do you ever pray specifically to one or the other or just to God in general?

_____

_____

If you find you relate to only one or the other, it's time for you to explore the basis of that. Some reasons are textbook examples, like mine coming from a broken home. Maybe you feel it's only reverent to speak to God as Father. I won't try and alter your beliefs if that is how you feel. I can only speak from my own circumstance.

I recently heard someone say that we can only pray to God the Father. His basis for that was the Lord's Prayer, which is a model not a directive. If we are expected to only pray that specific prayer, then how can we account for the fact that we are told to be wary of vain repetition in prayer? I admit, the man's statement sent me reeling since I was just about to write this chapter. Literally, I was to begin writing on this topic the following day.

I researched his position and came to my own conclusion. I found that some of my favorite pastors, Bible teachers, and commentators believe we can address Jesus in our prayers and even encourage it. Before the research, I said to my husband: "Good thing I didn't know I couldn't talk to Jesus all those years He was healing me." I was kidding, of course, but that truth did lead me to my primary reason to believe I can talk to Jesus directly: Even more than what other people said about how I can communicate with the Triune God, the proof of Jesus' intimate presence in my life and in my prayers was the miraculous transformation in me spiritually. I had prayed to Him, and He heard and healed me.

That may be what you need, miraculous transformation. In that case you must pursue an intimate relationship with both Father and Son. No matter the cost, chase after the One who chases after you. You will discover Him walking with you through your day-to-day life by His Holy Spirit.

"Then you will call upon Me and go and pray to Me,
and I will listen to you. And you will seek Me and
find Me, when you search for Me with all your heart."
(Jeremiah 29:12-13)

IN THE DAY TO DAY

"As the Father loved Me, I also have loved you;
abide in My love." (John 15:9)

True love isn't a feeling; it's an experience. Love is action. Love is listening. Love is there for you and cares for you. Love is a thousand little things. We live in a physical realm where spiritual things often remain hidden. After looking at the world around you and experiencing disappointment, rejection, and heartbreak, your eyes must adjust to the inner life of love you live with Jesus.

A verse has recently taken my heart captive. Jesus says in the Book of John that He and the Father would come and make their home with us (14:23). Consider that. The Father and Son are at home with you: in you, around you, beside you, before you, holding you. You are at home with the Person who is Love. You live out your life – all aspects of it – with God at home with you. No matter where you are or what you're doing, you can talk to Him. You can call on Him. You can reach for Him.

Instead of cohabitating with God, most settle for weekend visitation with Him at church on Sunday. For any kid from a divorced home, that feels all too familiar. We are comfortable with weekend visitation since we grew up with that life. Our experience has told us that is what it's supposed to be like with a dad. Since the divorce rate is around fifty percent, half the people who read this will know exactly what I'm talking about.

For those who have grown up with a dad in the home, you still may compare God to the distant dad you grew up with. And by the way, this isn't beat-up-on-your-dad day. Earthly parents get it wrong at times no matter their best intentions. It's just an observation that our minds are taught by our experience and sometimes, our perception of what we experienced. Then we act out what our minds believe.

The point is this: relationship requires investment, serious investment, on our part. There is an investment of time required in any relationship you value. Whether it's a marriage relationship, parent/child relationship, or even a friendship, you have to give of yourself and of your time in order for the relationship to grow. We invest in education, careers, and entertainment, but not in the Savior who came to save us.

The time you spend in pursuit of the Beloved is in direct relation to your closeness to Him.

After years of women's ministry, what I hear most is that women don't have time to devote to Bible reading and prayer. That's not true. They don't make time. There's a difference between having and making. Check on any one of those women's social media pages and, chances are, you'll find them pretty active. I'm not bashing social media. Just don't lie to yourself if you're using time as an excuse for a distant relationship with Jesus.

If you truly have no time to spend with God, then you have something on your plate God didn't put there. He would never order your life in such a way to where you couldn't spend time with Him. What father would do that?

Until God's love is experienced in the living out of your life, it won't feel real. It's in the everyday walk that love is proven. We give mental assent to the fact that God so loved the world that He sent His Son to die for us. But for some reason, we can't grasp the concept that God was just as intentional about sending His Son to LIVE out His life through us. Jesus, by His Spirit, is living in us and in our midst. He did die, but now He continues to live. Embrace that reality.

His love is ever-present. It's something you can feel and see and experience if you're paying attention. The morning God spoke the words *You. Are. Loved.*, I could actually grasp His love for me in a real and intimate way.

Here's the key as to why many miss His day-to-day love: They look for Him in the big things but not the little. I watch for him in nature and TV commercials and through His Word. I listen up when a preacher is preaching or a teacher is teaching. God's touch in my life comes in many ways. I'm ever watching and waiting.

Even if you have convinced yourself that God is present in your life, have you come to know that He is present in your day? Those are totally different thoughts.

In my life is the big picture.

In my day is the minutia of life.

We sing about Him being with us in the fire and in the flood, in the valleys and on mountain tops. When will we sing, "You're here with me while I wash dishes, sit in traffic, and fold laundry"? It's experiential love that transforms you – not head knowledge. It's seeing Him show up day after day. It's finding Him merciful when you blow it in the worst ways that assures you of His unconditional love. It's His whispers through His Word that stop you in your tracks. It ultimately becomes a staggering realization that God, the Almighty God that the Bible reveals, has shown up and is sitting next to you, giving you strength to face the day and peace to overcome the chaos. That's love! The One who is there, always, no matter if you woke up on the wrong side of the bed or if you are so weak and worn out you can hardly take another step forward. He's there. Love is pursuing you.

Question is, are you pursuing Him? That's what He wants, you know.

"And He has made from one blood every nation of men to dwell on all the face of the earth, and has determined their preappointed times and the boundaries of their dwellings, so that they should seek the Lord, in the hope

that they might grope for Him and find Him, though He
is not far from each one of us; for in Him we live and
move and have our being..." (Acts 17:26-28)

Notice it says He made us all so that we should seek Him. God is all about relationship with you. If you only knew the extent of relationship available to you, the difference it would make in your life, you would turn from chasing after the wind and chase after the Almighty!

If you do not currently devote time to this pursuit each day, it's time to begin. What you will find in His presence is worth more than all you currently devote your time to. Empty arms reach for the things of this world by default when not embracing Jesus. I don't even mean the bad things of this world. If you aren't full of Jesus each day, you will drink what the world offers.

I mentioned before about time being an issue for many believers. Is that the case for you? Do you struggle with setting aside time to spend with God?

Often, when someone says they don't have time, they underestimate the value of even fifteen to twenty minutes. If you set your alarm fifteen minutes earlier, you could read a small devotional and a few verses. That's a start. Or, if you're a night person, carve out a few minutes before you lay your head down.

I have to believe if you're reading this book then you want something different. You are longing for more out of your walk with Jesus. You need exactly what I said before, to walk with Him in the cool of the day. You want to feel loved. You want to experience closeness with Him. In that case it's time to change your approach. If you don't already meet with Jesus, starting tomorrow, find time. That's a loving directive from your sister. I don't care who in your family that inconveniences. Lock yourself in the bathroom with cotton balls in your ears if that's what it takes. That's a great mental image: you sittin' in the tub with your coffee, Bible, and rubber ducky with cotton balls stickin' outta your ears. Just do something. Make the first move.

The cool of the day for me is morning. I need strength to face the day ahead. I need the Bread of Life to nourish me. I need Living Water to face the parched world I live in, but schedules differ. You may be a night owl who needs to wash off the yuck of the world when you get home or before bed. What matters most is that you are actually setting aside that time. You won't likely know rest and peace if you don't. A strong truth is this: If you are at rest or at peace in this world without intimately walking with God, something is wrong. You can't know peace apart from God.

Ask yourself the following questions, not with condemnation, but just to take an honest inventory of your time.

How much time do you spend a day online and on social media? (Answer in minutes.)

Facebook _____   Pinterest _____

Instagram _____   Twitter _____

How much time each day do you spend on your phone? Texting, talking, surfing, and playing games? _____

TV time _____   Reading _____

Hobbies _____

We are all guilty of spending too much time on things that aren't necessary at the expense of that which matters most. Your time alone with God has to be a priority, or you will be stunted spiritually. I'm not creating a check list for you to do and become bound by legalism. I'm telling you a fact.

Time with God is how you get to know Him intimately. Time alone with Him is where love grows. You can't know you're loved if you don't know Love in the person of Jesus Christ.

41

If it were possible, I would come to each and every house and pull you out of bed, set your Bible in your lap, then pat you on the head and leave you in peace. It's what you need. Sadly, the enemy has fed you lies. He says you're too busy. He convinces you that fifteen extra minutes of sleep is better than walking with the God who created you. He deceives, and you eat. Nothing is more important than your walk with God. Nothing!

I remember a time in my early walk of faith when I didn't know what to do when I sat down to spend time with God. The Bible was intimidating. With so many concepts that seemed foreign to me, I was overwhelmed. Once I began structured Bible studies, that helped. I learned how to navigate around the many books of the Bible. I was asked questions that made me look up answers and fill in the blanks. In the absence of a study, what do you do?

It's as simple as: Read and Pray and Listen. For all the days of your life, these three things are how you communicate – both ways – with God. He speaks to you through His Word. You speak to Him in prayer. He often speaks to you through His Spirit. Your part is to set aside time and have a willing heart, one that will listen.

If having a quiet time is new for you, here are some helpful hints:

- Maintain a normal flow of reading. Where you end one day, begin there the next.

- Each day read one chapter of Proverbs. For example, on the fifteenth of the month, read Proverbs 15, on the next day Proverbs 16 and so on. The wisdom contained in this book will slowly seep into your belief system, and before you know it, you are making better choices based on what God says is wise living, not what the world says.

- Read through the Psalms.

- Start in Matthew and read through the New Testament.

- Try "red letter" reading. Slowly go through all the words of Jesus in the New Testament. Even when the stories seem familiar, reading Jesus' words specifically can take on a new dimension and speak to you in an entirely new way. Rather than your mind defaulting to the assumption that His words are directed toward others, you can feel them focused on you. Be advised, you may need to back up a sentence or two to gain context, but just as it sounds, you will pretty much stick to the red letters. Sometimes, as I read in this way, the realization washes over me – Jesus Himself is speaking to me, teaching me through the Holy Spirit. It's Supernatural!

- Begin at the beginning. Decide to read the Bible through. I would advise you, though, to move slowly. Avoid plans that require too many chapters or verses per day.

The goal is to have a place to begin each morning or evening. You will be surprised how He will speak to you as you read this way. Just read, even on those days when you "feel" as if you are not getting anything out of it. Commit to reading. Seeds are being planted. Remember, this is a marathon, not a sprint. Read small enough portions that you can study on it and allow the Spirit to speak. If you read more than a few chapters, you will not likely retain anything.

Some days, after a verse or two, I can't seem to move forward, which tells me that He has something for me to learn in those few verses. So I try to ponder and study on what I read, making sure I understand it or learn what He is trying to show me about Himself through it. Other days, I may take in several chapters. Sometimes I may not fully understand what I am reading at all or how it applies to me. In those times I have to believe that what I am reading is simply not for me in my current season. Then, years later, when the time is right, understanding comes as I read those same verses. The way He leads and teaches each of us may look different. For us all, though, there is one common denominator: we all have the need to meet with Him each day through His Word.

Other helpful tools:

- I use some kind of devotional almost every day. My favorite, the one I find myself going back to year after year, is *My Utmost for His Highest* by Oswald Chambers. I can't tell you the number of times it has spoken to my current need. It's deep, often way over my head, but I have found over the years that greater understanding comes as I have matured spiritually. There are loads of other daily devotions online and at local bookstores.

- Journal things you learn, things that stand out to you. Simply keep a spiral notebook near your Bible. When something really speaks to you, make a note of it. As you do this, you will begin to see common threads that the Lord is weaving into your heart. I promise, years later you will look back and be able to see your spiritual growth and trace the blossoming of your deepening relationship with Jesus. I also use my journal as a method of prayer. I find it helps to keep my prayers focused and on topic.

- Write favorite verses on index cards and keep them handy. (Thanks, Beth Moore!) I have stacks of verses that have meant so much to me during specific seasons.

- In addition to your normal Bible reading, listen to podcasts and read discipleship books. Expand your understanding a little at a time.

- Apply what you learn. That is where growth and change come, the application of a truth to your life. You can read every day, but until you learn to apply what you are learning to your daily life, you have accomplished little.

You. Are. Loved.

"But seek first the kingdom of God and His
righteousness, and all these things shall be added to you."
(Matthew 6:33)

The enemy speaks to you from his book of lies. Know the Book of Truth. The means of seeking God and His righteousness and kingdom is diving into Scripture for yourself. A pastor or teacher can never impart what your High Priest and Teacher can reveal. Replace lies with Truth and be transformed by the renewing of your mind (Romans 12:2).

Remember, if one thing doesn't work for you, don't give up. Keep trying. We all have to find our own groove when learning the dance of intimacy.

LOOK WITHIN:

Does your relationship with God resemble a weekend visitation or a day-to-day walk?

_____

_____

Do you notice that the time you spend with the Beloved directly relates to your closeness to Him?

_____

Do you invest time with Him, or have you relegated Scripture reading and prayer to a far-off corner of your life?

_____

Do you see God's activity in your life more in the big things or little? Give examples of each below:

Big:

_____

_____

_____

Little:

_____

_____

_____

Do you want something more alive and vibrant than you currently experience in your walk of faith? Devote the space below to what you want and how you think that would change your life.

_____

_____

_____

_____

What do you think it will take to get you there? What are you willing to add to your day in order to pursue this relationship and make your desire a reality?

_____

_____

_____

Pick one or two things from the lists above that might get you started in a consistent time alone with the Lord. Write them below and pray over your commitment.

_____

_____

_____

_____

PART TWO

LIVE THE LOVE SONG

Now that we are moving into the next phase, I want to revisit the love song and dance imagery and remind you:

His love is the music that draws us to the dance floor.
His Word guides our steps.
Our faith walk is the day-to-day dance.

In a physical sense, dance steps take practice. The more you hear the music, the more the song becomes a part of who you are and guides your steps. Internalizing the music helps the dance to take shape.

The same is true in the spiritual realm. The more you encounter God's love in your daily life (the music), the better you get at walking out your life of faith (the dance). Internalizing His love allows you to freely dance.

While you are practicing the dance, meaning each area of your faith walk, you will find the music of God's love grows only louder. As you continually turn your focus on the love of God in your day-to-day life, your steps will naturally align with the rhythm of His love. His love becomes more evident through your spiritual eyes and seeps like a haunting melody into your belief system, filling you with all the fullness of God.

"...to know the love of Christ which passes knowledge;
that you may be filled with all the fullness of God."
(Ephesians 3:19)

The ease of the dance is this: The real work is on God's shoulders. Your part is to show up each day with God and allow Him to lead you in the dance. Be patient. Keep practicing. Utilize the takeaway at the end of each of the following sections. It's frustrating to read a book and by the end lose track of all the key points that resonated with you. The takeaway will allow you to track your key points by topic.

In each stand-alone section, we will cover various attributes of what it looks like to live loved. Our ultimate goal is to be conformed to the likeness of Christ Jesus. I was well into working on this book when a thought came to mind Easter Sunday morning: Jesus knew He was loved by the Father and acted out of that love every moment of every day. He calls us to abide in that same love.

"As the Father loved Me, I also have loved you;
abide in My love." (John 15:9)

We can look at each of the topics in this book and see Jesus as our model. The question *What would Jesus do?* has become cliché, but it's still simplistic genius. Now we know the answer to that question – Jesus lived loved. It's more than us imitating what He did. It's who He is in us. We naturally live loved when we allow the holiness of Jesus to be exhibited in our lives. That comes from oneness with Him and from the sheer knowledge that He *is* love within us.

Outwardly, we can imitate anyone, a pastor or admired Bible teacher or friend. Inwardly, however, our motives may look nothing like that of our model. That was exactly me during my earliest walk, cleaned up on the outside but a hot mess in the deepest-down part of me.

While reading the topics to come, consider this a mirror to view (James 1:23-24). If you don't see your reflection in an area, then see it as a goal.

Paul says something compelling in Scripture about knowing Jesus and the power of His resurrection and fellowship of His sufferings:

*"Not that I have already attained, or am already
perfected; but I press on, that I may lay hold of that for
which Christ Jesus has also laid hold of me."*
(Philippians 3:12)

Paul, the author of more than twenty percent of the New
Testament, considered himself to be a work in progress. I'm just a
wife and mom and daughter, and here I am trying to express this vast
topic of living loved while still stumbling along on this journey. At
least Paul's admission gives us the assurance that we believers are all
pressing on toward a common goal together.

As you move through the following topics, you will be given an
opportunity to stop and ponder at the end of each one. Some topics
are brief; some are extensive, depending on the subject matter. You
will find overlaps in areas since each stand-alone section covers a
single theme. Principles that apply in one area may apply to others.
Many topics may have similar conclusions or takeaway concepts.
Case in point: I will always lead you to Scripture as the solution. If
that feels repetitive, then good. May I never be accused of thinking
I have the answers apart from God's Word. You shouldn't either.
Only God's Word is sharp enough to penetrate and divide soul and
spirit and judge the attitude of the heart (Hebrews 4:12).

When a topic resonates with you, take your time and consider
each area of the takeaway. Even if it takes days or weeks during your
quiet time, spend time praying and listening over that particular area.
Watch for ways God might communicate with you through His
Word, His Spirit, sermons, nature, and other believers. Illumination
will come.

I can't think of anyone who has mastered all of these areas, but
the mature believer continues working toward the goal of walking
with God well. The astute believer knows where they struggle, where
they need the most work, and they invest their time and attention to
making strides.

I have work yet to be done in every area, but what makes me
certain that God will accomplish the good work He's begun is

knowing I'm pliable. I am often willing to view myself as I really am, all my faults and shortcomings included. I've learned to consider myself with sober judgment.

"For by the grace given me I say to every one of you: Do
not think of yourself more highly than you ought, but
rather think of yourself with sober judgment,
in accordance with the measure of faith God has
given you." (Romans 12:3 NIV)

Are you able to do that? I don't mean beat yourself up over the little things. I mean, are you able to look deep within at your heart and motives? Introspection is key to each topic. If you can't or won't look at yourself soberly, you will likely never grow. For any of us, unless we admit where we are, we won't take the next step in our journey – we'll never learn to dance.

If you discover an attribute of living loved is missing from your daily life, it's time to take notice. There may be something hindering your trust in God's absolute love for you in that area. You need to begin to work with Jesus in your quiet time. Only time alone with God and learning the lyrics of his Word can bring the hindrance to light.

While working through the takeaway, if you feel a question doesn't apply to you, then ask God for confirmation. Once given, move on. Since I am a blank-filler-inner, I can stall out trying to look inward on a matter when it's simply not my season to direct attention to it. If that's the case with you and you feel it's not the time to explore something, move on to another topic. Here's the caveat, though, some issues you need to deal with can't be repaired until others are addressed.

Maybe you are hindered in an area due to some particular hurt from childhood or early adulthood. As an example: I shared earlier how the Gardener and I dug up some deep-rooted weeds from my life. My history of woundedness from my early years had me bound in nearly every area, especially that of trusting my Father. I needed healing from those wounds before trust finally came.

Until you trust God's love for you, many areas of growth will be hard to come by, especially ones which require you to step out in faith. In my case, trust came much later in my relationship with God. When it did come, it was the source of major transformation in every area of my life: parenting, ministry, and facing everyday life struggles. Answering my call was long overdue since I hadn't trusted the One calling. That is a good illustration of how one attribute, Live in Trust, is interwoven with another, Living Out Your Call. I didn't dream of stepping out in faith until I trusted God would catch me if I fell on my face.

Here's another case where healing had to occur before progress could be made in other areas. This one has an honesty alert attached! I love telling stories of miracles. This is one for sure:

After my fall and return to the Lord, I came back bound again by alcohol. It had been something that had gripped me for most of my adult life. My Christian friends had no idea I even drank since I hid it so well. It was a secret solace I ran to in order to quiet the chaos in my mind. My mind was so clouded by my self-medicating that little progress could be made toward my actual healing. Looking back now, I see why the Healer had to begin there. I needed a clear mind, a clean slate for God to work with.

When I had first begun to walk with God with any level of consistency, I stopped drinking without problem. It just happened that way, and I didn't give much thought to it. After my return, however, it wasn't that easy. I prayed for God to take the taste for it away. I begged. I kept trying to stop on my own, but still I drank.

One day on vacation at the beach, my favorite time to drink a cold beer, I opened one that tasted bad. Beer drinkers call it "skunk beer." I passed it to my husband who said it tasted fine. I opened another – same thing. It tasted just like a skunk smells. It struck me like a bolt of lightning. God had taken the taste away just as I had prayed, so I passed that beer off to my husband and haven't touched a drop since. Somehow, I know if I ever drink again I won't get another free pass. I will have to go the AA route like everyone else.

What's your skunk? What has you so hindered that progress can't be made in other areas? If you sniff around long enough – pun intended – you will smell it. Until you allow the Spirit to address and heal those issues, you won't make the progress you need. You, too, need a clear mind for God to work with.

Time to tackle our first topic. Like it was for me, for many, the first attribute we will cover is a stumbling block, a place where the relationship with God stalls. If that's the case with you, then it's time to take an honest appraisal of your heart and plan for the Love Song to play.

LIVE YOUR HEART'S DESIRE

"Delight yourself also in the LORD, and He shall give you the desires of your heart." (Psalm 37:4)

Before I take one step forward on this topic, let me remind you that "the heart is deceptive above all things, and desperately wicked" (Jeremiah 17:9). So before you go making plans to live out your heart's desire, you need to conduct a thorough heart check. You may find that your heart is in need of a recalibration.

A sanctified heart, one reshaped by Jesus, is a heart that can be trusted. That's a fact. A more realistic fact is that we are not yet fully sanctified, at least I know I'm not. I can't always trust my heart. I can't even often trust my heart. I have to be careful when following my heart or its desires. Why? Because this life has shaped my heart in such a way that my desires are for human relationships and approval. Yes, human relationships are vital for our well-being, but they should be secondary to our relationship with Jesus.

The more you grasp the greatness of God's love, the more it becomes clear that He is your greatest need and desire. As you grow in your love with and for Him, you must take inventory of your heart's current desires. What or who comes first? What is most prominent? There are many examples, specifically with human relationships where we can be off balance in our desires: the need for husband and mate kind of love and love for your children, parents, siblings, friends, and so on.

Let's focus on one area in particular: the love and desire for our (or a) man. That was once my own pitfall. Now, I'm in a healthy place where my husband is second only to Jesus, but that required me taking a sober look at my heart at its deepest level.

To establish my case, let's return to Eve in our story of the fall and its aftermath. Eve's original heart's desire was for relationship with God, but then the things of this world seemed more inviting. The serpent lied to her and convinced her that there was something more and that she was missing out. Next thing you know we are cussing Eve once a month and screaming in the delivery room. A part of the curse we don't often consider is this:

"To the woman He said: '...Your desire shall be for your husband, and he shall rule over you.' " (Genesis 3:16)

I can't count the number of times I've heard the part about "he shall rule over you" discussed when talking about the family structure. I honestly have no problem with this in our home. There are decisions that are deferred to my husband without hesitation on my part, especially when I'm too emotionally involved. Kelly has a level head in many areas where I don't. For the most part, though, we come to an agreement in all major decisions.

I want to camp at an all too underappreciated aspect of the curse. *"Your desire shall be for your husband."* Years ago, this struck me with fresh eyes. I can appreciate the magnitude of this desire considering it was once the most detrimental force in my life. Now, that curse over me is not only broken but totally demolished. Jesus is the unequaled desire of my heart, and growing my relationship with God the Father is absolute priority in my life.

That has taken years of being loved with a healthy God-shaped love. Prior to that, my desire was for a man, sometimes any man. My teens and early twenties were some of the most self-destructive years of my life. My view of love was skewed because my desire was skewed. I thought a relationship with a man was what would complete me. It didn't help that Jerry McGuire confirmed that with his broken plea to Dorothy (eye roll). I fell for it.

Movies and fairytales train us from the time we are little girls that we're waiting for our prince to come. I never knew I was waiting for my Prince in the person of Jesus. Romance novels only add to the idea that if we will just find Mr. Right then everything will be all right. And I say that as a writer and lover of love stories.

In any story I write, though, my heroine always comes to the place of needing the love of Jesus more than human love. It's usually the actual conflict to be resolved behind what seems to be the conflict. Why? Because in life that is the unresolved conflict with the woman's heart of flesh. She believes true love is horizontal rather than vertical. Some women are so desperate to love and be loved that they will settle for Mr. Right Now instead of waiting for Mr. Right. That may not be you, but if you've never been that girl, I bet you've known plenty of women like her over the years.

A thought occurs to me for the millionth time: Notice that the first of the Ten Commandments is to not have any other god before Him. The first part of the Greatest Commandment is to love Him with all our heart, soul, and mind. Everything else comes after vertical love – everything. Our love for others has its heathy basis in loving God and putting Him first.

That's not accidental. God knows the heart. If we jump back to our Jeremiah verse about the heart being wickedly deceptive, then we find in the very next verse:

"I, the LORD, search the heart, I test the mind."
(Jeremiah 17:10)

He knows what our hearts naturally desire, and He knows what our hearts supernaturally desire – Him. Good news: Jesus came to break sin's curse over our hearts. When you accepted Jesus as your Savior and the Holy Spirit took up residence in you, your heart's desire was recalibrated. Now, in the spiritual realm, Jesus is the desire of your heart whether you feel it or not.

In your flesh, however, you're still living under the curse. Remember, we were set up by the fairytale scenario. The prince kisses the princess and breaks the curse. She wakes up to happily ever after with her husband, right? Nope. There's no such thing as happily ever after with marriage. No matter the beauty of a healthy marriage, it's still not enough to complete us. We need the Prince. We need salvation and then for the desire of our hearts to shift to Him alone. Everything after that falls into line just like the Greatest Commandment depicts. We love others out of the overflow of our love for God. We love because God first loved us (1 John 4:19).

Okay, so what if that hasn't happened for you, loving God with your all? You wouldn't admit it to a soul, but what if your heart's desire is still for your man? There is nothing wrong with loving your husband. There's nothing wrong with wanting to be married if you're not. The point is: without a husband, are you lost?

We come back to this concept: Is Jesus enough for you?

I am wildly in love with my husband, something I couldn't have said years ago. We struggled so many of our first years that I finally gave up on loving him or being loved by him. Now that our marriage has been miraculously restored, I adore him. So I have to ask myself the same question: Without him would I be lost? In the physical sense, yes. We do everything together. I can't imagine going through life now without him. In a spiritual sense, though, I know I would be sustained by Jesus. I trust that. I've come to know such intimate healing over my worst wounds through my relationship with Him that I know He would be there to pick up the pieces if I were to be left a widow.

I've watched Him do that with my mom over the past few years. God has been there for her in every way she needs: Provider, Sustainer, Friend, Teacher, Father, and her Beloved. She has grown in spiritual ways that often surprise her. The loss of her husband wasn't her end as it felt at the time. It was the beginning of a new season with her Savior, one which allows her space to let Him claim her heart in new ways. She has seen God's love in action in her life and is now more vividly living loved because of it.

Desire for our (or a) man is both good and bad, light and dark. It can define and destroy. Unbalanced human love is a curse that must be broken. When considering the Greatest Commandment, note how Jesus says to love others after He says to love God. We can't know healthy love for others until our heart's desire is Him.

I will give you a peek into a journal entry of mine from the other day:

> "I think of my season of desperation and weeping before I knew You. I didn't hear it when You spoke my name, but my spirit did. Thank You for Your continual pursuit of me."

This wasn't referring to me before salvation. This was a reference to my fall and return. I didn't know Jesus as I do now. I didn't know His love and tenderness. I hadn't allowed grace to draw me deeper into Him. All along, the simplicity of God as the desire of my heart had been lost on me.

Some who will read this are in the same situation. Even if they haven't taken rebellious steps away from God, they are still far away in heart. Intimate life with Jesus isn't a reality to them. Their desire is still trained on physical relationships, especially with men. The concept of Jesus being their ultimate desire is a foreign one and may seem like some lofty, unobtainable goal. It seemed like that to me in my early years. Is that you?

This is a question we would all do well to ask in every season. Is Jesus the ultimate desire of my heart? Sneaky little foxes, as we are warned against in Song of Songs 2:15, can come and rob us of our true desire. Every day it would be wise to begin with this question: Today, Lord, are you the desire of my heart? What a great way to recalibrate your mind to start your day.

Is it possible that Jesus is speaking your name without you hearing? Is your spirit longing for a call your natural heart ignores?

The following encounter is one of the most tender examples of the intimacy Jesus shared with a woman who adored Him.

Mary stood outside the tomb of Jesus weeping when she saw two angels where the body of Jesus had lain. When asked why she was weeping, she said,

"Because they have taken away my Lord, and I do not know where they have laid Him." (John 20:13)

The story goes on to say that she turned around and saw Jesus but didn't know it was Him. That was me. Maybe that's why I am so affected by this story. I spent many years with Jesus as my Savior but never saw who He really was to me. He asked her,

"Woman, why are you weeping? Whom are you seeking?" (John 20:15)

The next part of the story is the most touching and personal aspect. Once Mary tells Jesus she is looking for her Lord, He says one word for her to recognize Him for who He is. He calls her by name.

Mary knew Jesus and the sound of His voice speaking her name. He had once cast seven demons from her. His earlier activity in Mary's life had created the most profound love imaginable, one that kept her Lord as her first priority even the morning after His death.

Beloved, you may not hear it with the clamor of the world distracting you, but He calls you by name so that you will see Him for who He is to you. He is the desire of your heart. No matter what you currently feel, prepare to embark on a journey to living your heart's true desire.

While gathering material for this section, I inadvertently turned to this verse when looking for the heart's desire passage. What a note to end with:

"May He grant you according to your heart's desire, and fulfill all your purpose." (Psalm 20:4)

If you will allow Him, he will be to you what you need. He will grant you the desire of your heart – Himself.

One thing that changed my relationship with Jesus was that I stopped praying to some far-away God and started praying to the next-to-me Jesus. In order to focus my mind and attention on the

Son of God, even now I close my eyes and imagine sitting in my favorite place, the beach. I speak to Him as if He's sitting next to me there. That's what I mean by the next-to-me Jesus. I consider the verse where He says, "Abide in Me, and I in you." He's ever present: within and without, beside and before. He's our rear guard and vanguard. He is always the next-to-me Jesus.

Now it's your turn. Talk to the next-to-you Jesus as you work through the questions below. Trust this process. Remember, it's during the exploration of what living loved should look like that you will find Him exploring right alongside you. How can you not feel loved by the next-to-you Jesus?

Preparing for your first Takeaway:

In the earlier chapters you were asked questions as a way to further consider each topic and look inward to get a glimpse of where your heart stands. Ongoing, you will find questions along with brief activities that will allow you to keep track of the chapter key points, engage with your Bible, and spend time in prayer.

It would be helpful to tear out and keep the takeaway as something to use during your quiet time and as you pray over an area of living the love song.

Remember, this journey with God is a life-long pursuit. Never stop seeking the deeper places with Him. Keep dancing, Beloved.

LIVE YOUR HEART'S DESIRE: TAKEAWAY

LOOK WITHIN:

Do you consider God to be close and approachable? Do you feel His presence as you sit with Him in the quiet place?

_____

You were asked two questions in the topic portion. Now, it's time to study them during your quiet time. No need to wear a mask. Be real before Him. Remember this verse?

"I, the LORD, search the heart, I test the mind."
(Jeremiah 17:10)

What or who comes first in your life?

_____

What would you consider your most prominent desire?

_____

Have you ever looked at your heart and its desires, knowing something must be off in your relationship with God? If so, in what ways?

_____

_____

_____

Have you been burned enough by your own desires where you now know the heart can't be trusted?

_____

After reading the material above, have you come to conclude that your heart may still be operating under the curse? Is your deepest desire still for human love no matter its form, husband, children, parents, etc.?

_____

_____

If your peek into your heart leaves you discouraged, take heart. What a beautiful jumping-off point for you, divine revelation through your time with Him that will result in your ultimate transformation. Be prepared for your Prince to come.

KEY POINTS:

- The curse is broken! The world has been lying to you. Human love isn't what your spiritual heart longs for.

- The more you grasp the greatness of God's love, the more it becomes clear that He is your greatest need and desire.

- Until you grow in your love with and for Him, you often need to take inventory of your heart's current desires.

PRACTICE THE DANCE:

How can you apply the Key Points of this section to your day-to-day life?

_____

_____

LEARN THE LYRICS:

- Look up Matthew 22:37.

We are commanded to love the Lord with all our:

_____

Where is your heart in relation to this passage? Focus on the word *all*, which indicates first place in every area.

_____

_____

_____

- Read John 20:15.

This is good question to ask yourself: Whom are you seeking? If not Jesus, what will it take for you to believe He is the One who completes?

_____

_____

_____

NEXT STEPS:

Ways to recalibrate the heart:

- Create a list of your hopes and desires in life. How many involve human love as the center?

- Take the next few days and pray over each individual area. Loving God first may not come naturally. Only the supernatural will realign your heart's priorities.

- Take a break from romance novels, movies, and secular music. Fill yourself, instead, with Scripture reading and worship music. Search for verses about God's love and faithfulness.

Your recalibrated heart is an attribute that will grow over time. If you don't now, you will come to love Jesus with all your heart, soul, and mind as you live out life in the day to day with Him.

STRIKES A CHORD:

What have you learned through this topic that requires further reflection?

_____

_____

_____

SING YOUR OWN SONG:

Through prayer, express where your heart currently is. Ask Jesus to teach you how to place Him above your desire for human love.

If you struggle with prayer, this may be a start:

Lord Jesus,
I want to love you with my all, but in its current state, my heart isn't able. I ask You to take my heart and make it Yours above all else. I invite You to come and invade my life and take my heart to be Your own possession.

LIVE THE LOVE LETTER

In the introduction I compared God's Word to the lyrics of His love song to you. When you know and experience God's active love in your life, you are naturally drawn to the words of the song. His lyrics are written in the form of a Love Letter, God's inspired Word in the collective work of the Holy Bible.

For many, the draw isn't there because His love doesn't feel real and personal. It will come in time if you are willing to take a step of faith and begin to read. There's a valid reason why each believer needs the Word of God: transformation.

> *"And do not be conformed to this world, but be transformed by the renewing of your mind, that you may prove what is that good and acceptable and perfect will of God."* (Romans 12:2)

Your life experiences have shaped your mind and thoughts. The way you were raised, where you were raised, events in your childhood and young adulthood, all these life experiences tell you who you are and what you feel. Many are lies. The serpent has deceived, and you have eaten. Those lies need to be dispelled with truth. The Bible speaks truth over those lies and tells you who you are and Whose you are.

No matter how your mind, feelings, and emotions have been shaped, whether negatively or positively, you still hear one call: "Come to Me..." (Matthew 11:28). That one phrase of the love song tells you all you need is to run to Jesus.

*"In the beginning was the Word, and the Word was
with God, and the Word was God."* (John 1:1)

In the passage above, John is referring to Jesus as the Word. So
when you read Scripture, you are in actuality getting to know Jesus
– *The* Word. The divine Book is His introduction of who He is and
how much He loves you.

Previously you were encouraged to pursue Jesus as the desire of
your heart. That's impossible to do without getting to know Him.
It's impossible not to love Him once you get to know Him in Spirit
and Truth.

Our verse from Romans about being transformed applies
here. None of this makes any sense at all without your mind being
renewed. The world-shaped, human brain can't grasp how we can
have someone who isn't physically present as the desire of our heart.
That's why this is difficult for women to believe. Our boyfriend,
husband, children, parents, and all the others who vie for our heart's
affection are living, breathing, walking-with-us beings. Horizontal
love relationships are something we can much more easily wrap our
minds around. But a faraway Jesus, how can we embrace Him?

If this was a natural process, I would stop here and list some
bullet points on how to know Jesus as your intimate companion, but
that's not at all how it works. The supernatural process of getting to
know Jesus is something that happens over time. At least it did for
me. My heart was only accustomed to accommodating human love,
so it fought against spiritual love for way too long.

In my own experience, I found that getting to know Him was an
incremental process that happened as I chose to meet with Him each
day. I would read something from the Bible or do a day's homework
in whatever Bible study I was attending and hope to hear something
that would apply to me. I noticed that something happened more
frequently. As I would read certain passages, it was like I couldn't
move beyond those words. Even if I did continue to read, the words
of what I was reading would never sink in because all I could think
of was the previous passage that had caught my attention.

Sometimes, that captivating passage would make sense, and I could see how it applied to me in my present situation. Other times, a verse would strike a chord, but I couldn't understand why. Here is one such example:

> *"No one engaged in warfare entangles himself with the affairs of this life, that he may please him who enlisted him as a soldier."* (2 Timothy 2:4)

I read this and couldn't read past it. I read it again and again. I fretted over what it might mean to me specifically since God seemed to have me stalled there. I prayed and asked, but revelation never came. A year or more later, I ran into someone who mentioned me coming back to work at my previous job. My first thought was that the spending money would be nice.

Bam! That verse came to mind. My understanding was finally opened. My call is ministry, in whatever form that takes. I knew I was supposed to pursue ministering to women and not that job. I wasn't to get entangled in the affairs of this life. When that passage originally caught my attention, God was giving me an answer to a question I wouldn't ask for another year.

Don't think I was some spiritual giant back when that verse stopped me in my tracks. Hardly! As a matter of fact, that was soon after my fall and return. I wasn't at all experienced in hearing from God through His Word, but that ended up being just one example of how He spoke to me through reading my Bible.

How did that help me to get to know Him better? I saw that He was actually present with me through His Word. He took an obscure verse and pinned it to my heart so that when the temptation came for me to take that job, illumination followed. I absolutely *knew* I wasn't supposed to say yes.

Though more than a decade has passed, when an opportunity comes up for me to consider a job outside of ministry, that verse comes to mind, and I know I'm supposed to keep doing what I'm doing.

Maybe that verse doesn't apply to you in the same way, but that isn't the point. I am hoping to give you an example of a practical application of living the love letter. As you practice this dance, you will have your own verses that grab hold of your attention and won't let go. It'll make sense when it happens but only to you.

When I think of the concept of getting to know Jesus, I think of a mail order bride. Two people meet from afar and send letters back and forth in order to get to know one another until the time comes to meet in person.

At first they are perfect strangers, but the more they read each other's words on paper or talk on the phone, the closer they become. They learn to recognize their intended's handwriting or detect certain inflections in tone. Anticipation and excitement builds until both can hardly wait for the day they begin to share a life together.

Jesus is called the Groom, and us collectively as believers the Bride. There will come a day when we will all meet him face-to-face. I don't want to meet a stranger. I want to know Him, what He sounds like, what it feels like to be with Him. That can begin now, even when it seems impossible as our Groom is with us only in Spirit.

Will you arrive in heaven someday and hardly know the One who laid down His life so that you could be His? If so, then you have to shift your current approach to your walk of faith. You absolutely have to invest in getting to know your Groom through His Word.

If you don't currently spend time reading the Love Letter and you consider doing that intimidating, take a step of faith and begin. He will lead the way and help you get to know Him. The supernatural part is His part. You don't have to figure it out. Girl, your only job is to show up each day. Allow Him access to your heart. Read. Study. Apply what you read to the best of your ability. Divine encounters will begin to happen. The first verse that speaks to an exact situation will blow your mind. Then it'll happen again. Then again. There will come a time when you open your Bible with the sure knowledge that Jesus will show up through His Word.

I can't remember where I read this phrase, but I think it's beautiful: breathless anticipation. There should come a day when you approach your time with Him with breathless anticipation. Isn't that what every longing heart desires, to come together with the one they love in breathless anticipation? This topic requires more depth than can be covered here, so this concept of expectation will overflow into our next section.

For now, let's shift our focus to a contrasting view of the Love Letter – your letter back to Jesus.

Years ago I began journaling. I'm not sure how others use a journal, but in mine I'm basically having a conversation with God. I address Him as "You" since I'm writing directly to Him. It's a focused way I pray. I also use the journal space to make note of things I've read and how He has led me in His Word.

If I tried to express the hundreds of ways He has led me to a perfect verse at the precise time I needed it, I would never be able to do it justice. There are times when I think a particular thought or have a question come to mind, then soon after, through some chain of events, I land at the exact verse that responds to that thought or question. That's no coincidence. I know it the moment I see it. I love to record those encounters.

I remind myself of the forgetful Israelites. I have these Wow! moments over the years and ask myself how I can ever doubt His intimate presence in my life again. Before you know it, I'm faced with a new challenge and find myself wondering if He will come through. Those are the times my journal comes in most handy. Since I often actually write the word *Wow!* beside some of my most notable God-sightings, when I glance back in my journals, those are the entries that catch my eye. Joshua would call those Stones of Remembrance.

This is my sixth book to write and publish. The others, being fiction, were entirely different animals. I didn't have much reason for doubt, other than wondering if they would be well-received. This book, however, keeps me doubting myself daily. I wonder if it will all come together as I envision it. I wonder what I'm thinking for even attempting it. I am on a mountain of inspiration one day and in the valley of doubt the next.

Recently, I have found myself so tossed back and forth that I have learned a new method of maintaining my resolve. I read back over one of my journals, the one that most represents this *You. Are. Loved.* journey. When I'm on the borderlands of doubt, I open my journal to some random page and begin looking for Wow! moments, those times when the Lord was so clearly leading the way toward this journey that doubt can't hinder me. It renews my strength so that I can soar again in belief.

I often wonder if other people are as bipolar in their spiritual moods as me. It's easy to see that King David was if you read the Psalms. Maybe that's why I retreat there often. When you read the chapters he penned, you will ride along with him through his highs and lows. Like David, I see the evidence of God and never, ever stop believing His goodness. Still, I need a glance back at times so that my current day's difficulties won't suck the wind out of my sails.

I can't recommend journaling enough. I recently heard a friend say that she wished people would stop trying to get her to journal. She feels it becomes a checklist, something she feels like she needs to do in order to check the box. The way I journal is nothing like that. If I have something I want to record, which is most days, I do. If not, I never feel bad about not writing.

Recently, I was trying to remember something from several years ago. I began to sift through old journals and scan the entries looking for that one particular thing. I came across one entry that got my attention. The date was there with this one line: "I'm hanging on by a thread here." That was it. I remember the season but not my exact woe. I just know that even when I was at my most discouraged, I wrote out my desperation in the form of my own love letter. I knew Who could pull me up from hanging off the ledge. He did.

Maybe looking at journaling differently will help you too. When God speaks to you through His Word, it can't hurt to respond in kind through your own love letter back to Him. Not only can you narrow in on your thoughts as you write, but you also are recording His goodness for later use.

I spoke on this topic recently, and a woman asked how I write personal things without fear of others reading what I write. Most of what I write anyone can see. For things more private, I'm vague in a you-know-who did you-know-what kind of way. When I read back later, I almost always know what my cryptic entries mean. I can tell by all that surrounds the season I was writing about.

She was wise to ask that question, and you would be wise to consider what someone would uncover if they read your journal. What if they find your love relationship with Jesus growing? That wouldn't be so bad.

Here is one more thought: There's this girl I know, After Nine Lisa. She's so negative and spends the last hours of the day trying to drag me down. I've learned to try and tune her out when she says I'm crazy for pursuing this writing ministry. Some nights, though, her voice is so loud that I believe the things she says.

I can hardly believe I'm on the mountaintop with Jesus at seven a. m., then I listen to After Nine Lisa insult me later that same night. I guess being tired after a long day makes me susceptible. A new way I've found to combat her is to scan my morning journal entry. It serves as a reminder of all the Lord spoke to me that morning. If I have nothing from the morning to read, or if my entry was on the negative side, then I have found that ending my day with a quick entry of thanks for the day can hush After Nine Lisa.

Journaling doesn't have to look like anything in particular. Find what works for you. I just know from experience that having a record of all that God has done, your prayers and praises, and how your closeness with Him has grown, can have power over doubt.

Scripture along with prayer and journaling back to Him has explosive power. His Word to you and yours back to Him are like singing a duet, a beautiful new love song every morning. If you don't feel naturally drawn to read, give it time. Until you do, you will have to walk (and read) in faith that He will whisper His love over you.

LIVE THE LOVE LETTER: TAKEAWAY

LOOK WITHIN:

How has the world shaped your mind regarding your belief in who Jesus is?

_____

_____

We act out of what we believe. If we are convinced that intimacy with Jesus isn't something we can attain, then we will never seek Him with our whole heart (Psalm 9:10). What heart attitudes and mindsets do you believe need to be transformed within you?

_____

Does the fact that Jesus is with you in Spirit rather than physically make intimacy with Him seem unbelievable?

_____

Do you believe the Bible is God's infallible Word to you, His Love Letter to introduce Himself to you?

_____

List one or two areas where you are actively inviting God in to do a mighty work.

_____

_____

Do you have an example where a Bible passage spoke directly to you?

_____

_____

If you don't, plan to encounter your own Word from Him when you choose to begin to read the Bible consistently. He is faithful. He does speak.

KEY POINTS:

- The world has misshaped our minds and hearts.

- Lies are combatted by the truth of God's Word.

- Our minds are renewed through Scripture reading.

PRACTICE THE DANCE:

How can you apply the Key Points of this section to your day-to-day life?

_____

_____

LEARN THE LYRICS:

- Write Matthew 11:28 below.

_____

This is a key scripture that would benefit you to remember each day. Write it out on an index card as your reminder that He will carry your heaviest burden and give you rest.

You. Are. Loved.

- John 1:1 calls Jesus the Word.

What correlation does that have with us spending time reading the Love Letter?

_____

_____

NEXT STEPS:

- Commit to a quiet time reading each day. Don't stress over reading long passages. If you only read a few verses and then ponder what you've read, you will find a renewal of your mind begin to take place. Be patient as you learn to navigate your Bible.

- Commit to applying what you read. If you feel the sting of conviction in an area, don't allow pride to prevent your obedience.

- Try a journal entry or two. Use the space for a conversation directed to the Lord. Find your own groove. You may be a morning person or night person. You may be long winded, or a few short words might make your point. Allow yourself the freedom to make your journal look any way you want. Your entries should reflect you.

- Keep track of significant verses. Record insights and questions. Write out entire verses in your journal so that when you go back and read, you have the context of the verse already there for you.

- Write outside the lines of your journal. Make notes in your margins next to jaw-dropping revelations. When something touches my heart, I will draw a little heart next to an entry or a smiley face. I have even made a copy of a devotional entry and taped it onto a journal page.

STRIKES A CHORD:

What have you learned through this topic that requires further reflection?

_____

_____

_____

OUT OF TUNE:

Are there areas of your life that are out of balance with God's Word? These may be actions, attitudes, or hidden places in your heart you are withholding from His touch. If so, will you commit to pray and allow His truth to dispel any lies you are holding onto?

_____

_____

SING YOUR OWN SONG:

Praying God's Word back to Him is a powerful song. Find verses that mean something to you and turn them into prayers.

Example:
I ask, Lord, that You make your Word come alive and have power in my life. I ask that you divide soul and spirit and look within the depths of me (Hebrews 4:12). I want to be transformed by the renewing of my mind (Romans 12:2).

LIVE IN EXPECTATION

The room is dimly lit in the wee hours of the morning. The sun is only partially up, casting just enough light as you step out onto the dance floor and wait for the Words of the song to begin. This is the dance of expectation, one of knowing your partner will arrive and speak with a still small voice as you read His Word.

Expect to encounter Jesus, the Word made flesh. He longs to speak to you. Expect long-term transformation as your mind becomes renewed. This isn't an overnight process, and learning to navigate your Bible will take time, but you can believe you will learn and grow and begin to detect the sound of His voice as you show up each day. That must be your commitment of faith in the beginning, reading and learning the lyrics of God's love song, His Word. The ability to hear and follow His lead will develop as you get to know the One who calls you away to dance the dance in a quiet place with Him.

At first it's all so overwhelming with new concepts to learn and apply. I remember well what that felt like. My very first women's study was *A Heart Like His* by Beth Moore, a study of King David.

Once when I was watching one of the session videos, I looked around the room and wondered if the other women there had a clue what Beth was talking about. Bible-talk was all new to me then. I felt stupid for not knowing what she was talking about and too proud to ask someone to help me learn. Part of me feels my stubborn pride was a hindrance, but part of me is glad I allowed the Spirit to be my teacher. I'm sure it took longer for me to learn without help, but the lessons I've learned over the years have sure stuck.

One thing I committed to do was the homework. I noticed how other women would come in and say they just didn't have time. I know we all get busy, but I have to say that investing time in reading the material, looking up the verses, and filling in the blanks to the best of my ability made a huge impact.

I don't want to see anyone shy away from reading their Bible because it seems too intimidating. If you're brand-spanking new, try to stick to story related chapters. Genesis and Exodus set the stage for the Patriarchs and tell you of Moses and his impact on the people of God. Joshua will help you cross over into the Promised Land with the people of God. Esther's story will captivate your romantic heart as she becomes an unlikely queen. Her willingness to risk her life for God's purpose and people will take your breath away.

The prophet books like Isaiah, Jeremiah, and Ezekiel will throw you for a loop early on. Maybe hold off on those until you take a study with a teacher who will guide you through. And Revelation? That'll curl your toes. They are all amazing books that declare God's faithfulness, but at first they might seem overwhelming.

It doesn't matter your experience with reading your Bible; we are all on equal footing as believers. We have the Holy Spirit within, the Author of the Book who will open up our understanding.

> *"These things I have spoken to you while being present with you. But the Helper, the Holy Spirit, whom the Father will send in My name, He will teach you all things, and bring to your remembrance all things that I said to you." (John 14:25-26)*

One key thing I discovered while learning to read my Bible: I didn't have the capacity to figure things out. It was up to the Spirit to open my understanding. There is a big difference. Only the Spirit can illuminate a verse that seems a mystery. Sometimes, I never know what something means, but I have to believe it's just not for me to know. I don't have to know it all, just what it takes for me to follow Jesus faithfully.

Here are a few things you can expect as you begin to read your Bible more often:

You will grow in understanding.

Along with a deeper knowledge of the milk of your faith, which is God's love, you will learn new and more challenging concepts while reading. You will be addressed in ways that are unique to you regarding areas where you need to shift your attitude.

Case in point: Me and my mouth. I can have a sharp tongue. When I first began to read my Bible with any regularity, I was constantly challenged to watch my mouth. Actually, today would have been a great day to have been challenged. I lost my cool with someone I love dearly and said some things I should have kept silent about. I kept telling myself how right I was on the matter and just kept spewing hurtful things. It didn't matter if I was right or not. I was wrong for my brutal words. I can't take them back now.

If I'm perfectly honest, I did receive a word through Scripture just this morning. It wasn't a passage that spoke specifically about the mouth, but it was clear enough that it applied to my situation and should have defused what became a heated exchange. Had I heeded the warning, I wouldn't have said the things I did. That's why applying what we read matters. I didn't today. I regret that. I can only be thankful that God's mercies are new every morning (Lamentations 3:22-23).

Your faith will grow deeper.

The more you see the truth of Scripture come to life and be proven in and around you, the more faith you will have to lean on. When you read something that challenges you to take a step of faith in obedience, and you choose to do it, you will find God faithful. It may not be right away that you see the outcome you hoped for, but time will almost always show you your step of faith was exactly God's plan for you at the time. It's often easier to see that in hindsight than while walking out the step.

If you poll mature believers who have consistently taken faith steps, you will be hard pressed to find many who will later say they regret their obedience. Most will say the opposite, that even what seemed like a failure at the time God used in a way He couldn't have if they had not taken the step.

Looking back at my own history, there were times when I stepped out in faith and felt like it was a disaster. Just like every other less-than-mature believer, I blamed God. I asked all the usual questions: Where were you? I thought you said to… How could you let me fall?

In every case I can now look back and see my faith step was rewarded and was exactly His plan for spiritual growth at the time. It sure didn't feel like it then, but His plan was always better than mine.

I once taught a class that seemed like nothing less than a disaster at the time. I never felt prepared enough. At the time I gave it the best I had to give, which wasn't much with my level of spiritual maturity. All these years later I can see that class as my entry point into the current ministry I now know. I formed bonds that will be life-long. I hope I made a small impact on those young lives. What mattered was that I was faithful to obey what I knew to be God's leading.

I tell you that for this reason: Take steps of faith. Whatever the outcome, your success lies is in your obedience. If God is calling you to trust Him enough to step out in faith, then rest assured He will either catch you if you fall or teach you invaluable lessons when you land. I will never pretend to understand God's ways. I do know this, though: He is good. Whatever His methods, His way is the right way.

Inner healing will take place.

I've mentioned before how broken I was when I first began my true pursuit of Jesus. At the time I actually had no idea how damaged I was in my emotions and my way of viewing life. I found, though, that the more I read truth, the more I recognized the lies I had believed. The more I read of God's love for me, the more I was willing to open myself up to that love.

There's a verse I claimed as my own many years ago:

"He sent forth His word and healed them."
(Psalm 107:20 NIV)

My miraculous transformation and subsequent use by God can be explained by no other means than His Word healing my wounded soul. I can't express enough or implore you enough to seek healing through God's Word. No matter the collateral damage done in your life by the world's warfare, healing is found only through Jesus as He tends to your wounded soul.

Healing takes time. A lifetime of wounds requires the Great Physician. There is something about the lasting effects of childhood and young adulthood trauma that lingers in a way only those who experience it can understand. It remains so ever-present that over time the enemy convinces you that your wounds are part of who you are. That isn't true at all. Jesus came to heal the brokenhearted and proclaim liberty to the captives. If your past hurts hold you captive, Jesus is your liberator (Isaiah 61). Plan to spend time in that power-packed chapter in your takeaway. My Bible is marked up with all kinds of notes along the margin of that particular passage.

What stands out most to me now is "the after" statements. It's as if verses 1-3 depict the healing and transformation of the believer. Then in the latter part of verse 3 and following we find out the "what for."

"That they may be called trees of righteousness, the planting of the LORD, that He may be glorified. And they shall rebuild the old ruins..." (Isaiah 61:3-4)

There is a reason for God to spend time on your healing. He has a plan for you, that you will glorify Him through your transformed life. If anyone is proof of His healing power, I am. I say this with all sincerity: I have no idea why He is choosing to use someone with a past such as mine. Maybe he is using me *because* of my past. What better way for God to receive glory than to turn Old Lisa into this new version of myself, a woman who loves Him with all her heart, soul, and mind, a woman who will shout His love from the rooftops to anyone who will listen.

He has a plan for you. Don't ever doubt that.

He will speak clearly and precisely.

The more you read, the more you will learn to hear from God as He speaks into your life and circumstances. You will find His voice comes in gentle and not-so-gentle ways. Your topic takeaway will direct you to 1 Kings 19:1-13 for a great example of how God spoke to Elijah through what is called a still small voice (vs. 12).

More often than not, I find that's how God speaks to me. While reading Scripture, there may be exactly that, a still small voice that convicts or directs or reminds me that I am loved and protected.

Other times His response to a question or concern can be so out-loud that I have no confusion over what He has to say to me. One of my favorite examples of God speaking directly to me through the obscurest of verses is this:

I found a show called *Madmen* and watched a few episodes. It was about the behind-the-scenes life of advertising executives. Those first few episodes weren't so bad. At least infidelity was accurately portrayed in that there were consequences for the cheater. Then something happened on one episode that made my eyes nearly pop out of my head. The act wasn't actually shown, but what was insinuated was sexually graphic, almost to the point of a violent assault.

That scene so stayed with me that I even woke the next morning with the image burned into my mind. Before beginning my quiet time that morning, I half-heartedly whispered, "Lord, I don't think I need to watch that show anymore."

The reason my statement was half-hearted was that, knowing myself, I liked the show so much that I could have easily discounted that one thing considering the show wasn't bad overall.

Yeah, that didn't happen.

I opened my Bible to Jeremiah, where I just happened to be in my normal flow of reading. When I picked up where I had left off, this verse was there waiting in response to my statement:

"You too, O Madmen, will be silenced."
(Jeremiah 48:2 NIV)

I have never seen a more blatant and direct response by God. I nearly threw my Bible when I read that. Come to find out, Madmen was the name of a city, but that was beside the point. Needless to say, I never watched that show again.

When I say God speaks in not-so-gentle ways, my Madmen verse is a great example. His Word to me cracked like thunder that morning. That too was a good example of why maintaining a normal flow of reading is beneficial. When you get a word specific to your situation, you are able to see God as the strategic genius that He is. Also, you see how intentional He is to be present in the details of your life – even your TV watching choices.

Just a note, here: If you watched that show, I'm not beating you up at all. That one instance may very well have been isolated. For me, though, I have to take great care with what I watch when it includes anything sexually inclined. With my past of sexual abuse and later sexual sin, it's just not where my mind needs to dwell.

Questions will be answered.

In Proverbs 3:5-6, we are told:

- Trust in the LORD with all our hearts

- Lean not on our own understanding

- Acknowledge Him in all our ways

- He will direct our path

When you have little and large life questions, ask them. God wants to guide and direct you. He's your Father. Why wouldn't he answer when you ask? Notice, though, those first three points. They provide what seems to be a key to hearing His direction.

First, we need to trust Him enough to follow. When we ask His direction, we need to be prepared to do what He says.

Second, His direction often flies in the face of conventional wisdom. And it almost always differs from what the social expectations of the world around you say. Sex outside of marriage is a great example. Everyone does it now, right? Sadly, yes, even professing Christians. As a Christian fiction author, I find it difficult to write characters who wait for marriage, not because of what I believe, but because even Christians nowadays consider not waiting the norm. It's difficult to make it believable that a young woman in her twenties could still be a virgin.

If you are single and ask God His direction on that topic, His answer will be to wait. No matter what you feel. No matter what everyone else thinks, God's best for you is to wait until marriage.

Third, acknowledging God in all our ways seems like a vague statement, but it's actually pretty specific. It means all, not some, not the ones that match our viewpoint. All means all.

I bring this verse and all its parts into focus for this reason: God answers questions for those who want to hear His answers. It's those who want to pick and choose the answers and their obedience to them who struggle with hearing Him.

Your mind will be transformed.

Several times already I have discussed how the world we live in has shaped our minds, so I won't spend much time here. I will say this: If you have attempted to read Scripture before and found yourself frustrated enough to quit, then give it another try. Approach your reading with a new attitude, knowing that it will take time for your spiritual eyes to focus.

I hope the suggestions I gave you before about sticking with some of the story-based chapters will help. For goodness sake, Leviticus can wait awhile. If you decide to read the Bible through from beginning to end, you may get bogged down in some of those earlier chapters. It's okay to begin where you are comfortable enough to stay the course. Just don't stay in the shallows forever. The deep end with God is where I've grown and been challenged in inexpressible ways. Like Jeremiah, for example, steering me away from a show that wasn't God's best for me.

There are innumerable treasures you will find in Scripture. You will find stories of: intrigue, infidelity, faith walks and falls, expulsions and invitations, rises to and falls from power. There is no literature on earth with the power contained in this precious Love Letter written to God's Beloved. Your attitude when approaching your time to read affects the outcome of your experience. Expect little and receive little. Expect much and receive much.

You will hide His Word in your heart.

The more time you invest in reading, the more God's Word will seep into your thinking and come to you when you need it most. You have likely been told this so many times that you find yourself ignoring it: you should be memorizing verses. I mentioned in the Day to Day chapter some suggestions to get you started, like reading plans and ways to get familiar with your Bible. Memorizing God's Word is the act of drawing the Word within you. Consider the written Word God's exhale and memorizing your inhale.

What I consider memorization is different than most people. Their goal is to get the exact words down pat so that they can quote it word-for-word. My goal is to draw the essence of the verse into my mind and absorb it into my understanding.

The reason I am more concerned with the essence rather than the exact word, is that focusing on exact words can become more of a check list toward perfection. The goal is to apply the meaning of the verse in my heart and life. Too, versions differ. I read so many different versions, I can't possibly know every one down to the last word. I would much rather know what God is saying than the words man has used to translate. This may not be your way of doing things, but I genuinely believe God's truest desire is for us to absorb His heart on the matter rather than the exact words.

To live in expectation means you know God loves you and you know that His love will speak and guide those who read His Love Letter. When He speaks to your heart through Scripture, whether through a whisper or crack of thunder, claim that verse as your own. I shared the verse about His sending forth His Word and healing me. Your own specific-to-you verses will come and will soon begin to accumulate in number. I now have many special verses after these years pursuing God through His Word. When certain situations arise, a verse comes to my mind and answers a question I haven't even thought to ask. It will do the same for you in time. Remember, your job is to show up. His job is to claim your heart and transform your mind.

LIVE IN EXPECTATION: TAKEAWAY

LOOK WITHIN:

Do you have a long history with Bible language, or is it a mystery to you?

_____

Have you participated in Bible studies? If not, do you think it would benefit you to join one?

_____

Psalm 32:8 tells us that God will instruct and teach us in the way we should go. When you read your Bible, do you feel the leading of God through what you read? Give an example.

_____

_____

How has your personal faith grown deeper through steps of faith? List as many examples as you can think of.

_____

_____

How can Scripture transform a world-shaped mind?

_____

_____

KEY POINTS:

When you study God's Word, you can expect:

- You will grow in understanding.
- Your faith will grow deeper.
- Healing will take place.
- He will speak clearly and precisely.
- Questions will be answered.
- Your mind will be transformed.
- You will hide His Word in your heart.

If you don't currently experience these things, then you have encountered a roadblock that requires prayer. Ask God what is standing in your way. Don't be afraid to reach out to a trusted friend, pastor, or Bible teacher to discuss your concerns.

PRACTICE THE DANCE:

How can you apply the Key Points of this section to your day-to-day life?

_____

_____

LEARN THE LYRICS:

- Read Psalm 107:20.

List areas in which you have been healed by the Word of God. If you can't think of any, list areas where you are seeking His healing.

_____

_____

- Read Isaiah 61 line by line. Envision yourself as the topic of conversation. Examples: Jesus came to heal your broken heart. He came to set you free. Use this as an opportunity to journal your thoughts and prayers.

- Read 1 Kings 19:1-13.

In what ways did Elijah expect to hear from God?

_____

Instead, how did God speak?

_____

How has God spoken to you through a still small voice?

_____

_____

_____

NEXT STEPS:

- Take a chance on joining a women's Bible study. You will grow in immeasurable ways through meeting with others and discussing what you are reading and learning.

- Through prayer, begin to ask questions of God. Then expect God to answer.

- Allow God to ask you questions. Like He asked Elijah in our 1 Kings passage, He asks similar questions that He wants you to consider. "What are you doing here?" is a question He asks. What is your answer to that question? What is it that you are seeking from Him? Journal your thoughts.

- Begin to truly study – not just read Scripture. Absorb what you read into your mind and heart.

STRIKES A CHORD:

What have you learned through this topic that requires further reflection?

_____

_____

_____

SING YOUR OWN SONG:

Write out a prayer that reflects your heart. Do you come to meet with Jesus in expectation? If not, ask Him to open your heart and help you learn to trust that His presence is with you.

_____

_____

_____

Journal your questions. As God begins to answer you through various ways: Scripture reading, sermons, or what others may say to you, update your journal with what you believe is God's answer. Keep your line of communication open.

LIVE OUT OF CONTROL

*"The LORD sat enthroned at the flood, and the LORD
sits as King forever."* (Psalm 29:10)

Where some dances are quiet and filled with grace and beauty, others consist of lumbering steps and unfamiliar rhythms. Sometimes we can hardly hear the music and can't help but wonder if our Partner is there and leading the way. What can you hold onto and whose hand can you hold when forced to dance a dance so out of your control? The King who extends His arms and invites you to trust the One who loves you.

Psalm 29 abounds with imagery of God's glory and sovereignty. This verse reminds us that when the greatest world-wide natural disaster in history occurred, God was in control. And now, He still sits as King over every flood, our floods of personal disaster included. Before reading on, I urge you to stop and read the entire Psalm for yourself as a reminder that God is in control and can be trusted to bless His people with peace (vs. 11).

For us as believers, control is an illusion. Why then do we fight for control in an out-of-control world? Isn't the basis of sin exactly that – the desire to be our own god and control our lives?

The root of my own need for control is easily traced back to feeling a lack of control when I was a little girl. That led to a woman whose goal in life is to control her surroundings and even the people she loves – for their own good, of course.

It has taken me decades to discover this one unchangeable fact: Control is an illusion. We grip those closest to us and cling to the premise that if we love deeply enough, if we give all that they need,

93

they will be okay and life will turn out right. Come to find out, that's not how it works at all. The more tightly you grip someone, the more they squirm to get away.

There's an innate desire in humanity for justice, well, in much of humanity. It begins as little children as they cry out, "That's not fair." Ultimately, life isn't fair. Circumstances don't turn out as we hope, as we pray. Early in my walk of faith, I held the belief that if I just prayed hard enough over something, God would answer as I wanted. Sometimes that has been the case, but in some of my most desperate pleas, my prayers weren't answered as I had hoped. In many cases, when looking back with hindsight, I can see God's better plan than what I had asked for. In others, however, I still can't see the good in the outcome.

I was recently on what I felt to be a mountaintop, then next thing I knew, there I was flat on my back in the valley. I've struggled to climb the walls and get myself out of this dark place. Each day I promise myself that the next day will get better, that I will handle this all better, but I'm lying to myself. Nothing is better. I'm not better.

There are areas in my life that are totally out of my control. No matter how much I fret or worry, I can't do one thing to change them. Something hovers overhead, constantly threatening to crush me. So what do I do? I put my trust in God. Not in a lip service way but in a heart-wrenching, help me take the next breath kind of way. At times, when looking at this situation, I don't see how a Sovereign God could be in control and not do something to change it. He hasn't yet. He may never.

All I can do is glance back at how He has always come through – even when all hope seemed lost. There have been plenty of times when He didn't show up like I had hoped or prayed for, but my backward glance assures me He was still in control, and I can see how He has made beauty come from the ash heaps of my own past. He will do the same thing in the situation I'm hurting over.

Ever the optimist, I have to wonder if the reason for the fall from the mountain is so that I can write this chapter with true, up-to-the-moment raw emotion. Many times, when writing about spiritual truths, I can look back at my history with God and how He taught me and then discuss those principles analytically. Allow me to be in the throes of living out the truth when it's most difficult, and I'm all over the place emotionally. I'm up one day and in a pit the next. But "in the throes" is exactly where I'm writing from now. To try and pour out truth when I'm barely living it is one of the most difficult tasks I've ever undertaken as a writer.

I woke this morning somewhere in the middle of my emotional roller coaster, neither at the top or bottom. What I am doing is choosing to live out of what I *know* today rather than what I feel. That's the only solution when things are most difficult and God seems less than in control. I have a choice to make: Do I doubt Him and try to take over the situation in which He seems absent, or do I be still and know that He is God? Each day I get that same choice. So far, I have remained still. Don't get me wrong, I have opened my mouth or started typing a message that would prompt a conversation that I wasn't sure I should have. Each time the reminder came that because I still didn't know the right course, I was to do nothing.

The old me tries to convince the redeemed me that if I can just say enough or do enough, then I can get things back on track. The truth is, there doesn't seem to be a "back on track" in this situation. It's a new normal that I will have to learn to live with. Maybe that's where I'm so stuck. I don't want this. I can't process it clearly. It is out of my control. For me that's simply unthinkable.

Enter God, a sovereign God who's been on His throne from the very beginning. He has had and still does have a plan, and His plan is better than my own, even when I can't see it now, even when the situation is too painful for words to express.

There is a word in the Christian faith that's underutilized, undervalued, and often under spoken with sincerity: Lord. Sure, we consider Him our God and Savior, our Shepherd and King, but Jesus as Lord isn't something we want to live with. What if His plans don't match up with ours? When we are told to confess Jesus as Lord, that's not just some one-time proclamation as found in

Romans 10:9. It is a life confession as found between Jesus and Peter in Matthew 16:13-18 where Peter declares that he knows Jesus is the Christ. Jesus is either our Lord and we follow and believe, or we have taken a step away in order to be our own (little g) god.

I choose Him as Lord over this situation that is so out of my control. I do not choose out of blind obedience, though that would be enough. I call Him Lord because of all I have experienced in the past. I have a history with Him that defines my present and future. Why would He fail me now? I can see the consistent pattern of His goodness, even amidst my worst tragedies. Why would He give up and walk away now?

Please hear me. Hear my heart. This situation I'm going through is the exact thing that I've dreaded for several years now and built up in my mind as the worst that could happen. I've waited for it, prayed against it, and now here it is. At times I just refuse to think about it at all and walk in denial. Other times it's so prevalent that nothing else can penetrate my mind because it's filled with fear and grief and disappointment. Some days I'm stuck. Some days I have enough faith to keep me going. Right now, this very second as I write, I'm sitting in bed with my comfy pink robe on simply because I don't want to do anything else. It would be easier today to pull the covers up over my head and allow depression and heartbreak to chart my course. Instead, I have chosen to pour out my sincerest thoughts here. Next, I will choose to hit the shower and go to church. I need corporate worship today. I need a man of God to pour truth into my grief-filled spirit. I need Jesus today.

Earlier I said I choose to allow Jesus to be Lord over this situation. We all get that choice. You, right now as you're reading this, may have that "worst that could happen" situation glaring at you. You get to choose. Is He your Lord? Or will you cast Him aside, take the reins, and drive over a cliff?

If you choose to allow Him to be Lord over your storm, what do you do? What are your next steps? Since I am watching flood waters rising in my very own life, I will share with you three things that are helping me hold on to the hope that He is God over the flood: Be still. Be honest. Believe.

Be Still

In one particular aspect of my situation, my brain says to move, but I still have a check in my spirit. Usually when I have a sense of restraint, I know it's God saying not to move. I'm not so sure this time. The steps I am to take are ones I don't want to take. Sure, I'm willing if that's what obedience requires of me, but I just don't know. I keep doubting myself, thinking maybe the hesitation I feel is fear trying to prevent me from doing what I believe needs to be done rather than spiritual restraint. I have to clarify before I act: is this fear or is this faith?

I know this isn't just a me thing. No matter how many years any of us walk with God, I have to believe we all bump into this roadblock. At times His leading isn't clear. What seems right just doesn't feel right deep down. So what do we do when what's happening externally and what's causing turmoil in our spirit collide? Do we take a step forward in uncertainty?

What we should do is trust Him to confirm when the time is right. In my case I have listened to the quiet whisper to wait, to believe the Spirit has been holding me back. For weeks I did nothing until I finally began to suspect that maybe it was actually fear creating the hesitation. One morning this past week, when I was to the point of desperation, I told God that I didn't trust myself to believe I had heard Him tell me to wait. I was going to take the steps that seemed to make sense.

Within moments of that prayer, I opened my Bible to the place where I had left off the morning before. Of course it was Psalm 46:10 that told me to "Be still, and know that He is God." I say of course because God is really God. He knew where I would be mentally that morning and that I would need His written reminder to wait, to be still.

I'm not sure if this will help anyone but me today, but as I recount this story, it serves as my reminder that I am fully prepared to be obedient. If that means proceed, I will proceed. If that means wait, I will wait. Since everything points to the wait, even when conventional wisdom says proceed, I will wait. I will do nothing and say nothing. If I'm wrong, if I discover I have handled this badly in the long run, I have to stand on the principle of faith that I have done what I believe God is calling me to do in the moment. I pray that my faith will be credited to me as righteousness.

This walk of faith isn't easy. It's rarely black and white, especially when the crazed world around you hits you with shades of gray. When all you see around you seems out of control, you are left with this: God is in control and sits as King forever.

Be Real

In your prayer life, decide to be real. Discuss how you feel with God. Express your disappointment. Share if you feel hurt. Ask Him to give you scriptures to lean on, ones that will bring you peace. Shallow prayer will keep you wading in the shallows. Plumb the depths with the Lord.

Recently, I've come to a place with Him that leaves me saying, "I don't understand why You haven't intervened, but I trust You anyway." If it were anyone else going through this, I would have an objective answer to give them: For God to intervene in this situation, He would have to negate the will of another. Hasn't that been the theme all along, even before Adam and Eve made the choice to sin? God gives man free will. Love demands nothing less. God isn't a caring Father if He ties his children up as puppets and dances them around in accordance with His will. We, as His children, get to choose our own path, even when it's in error, even when our actions toss others into a valley.

Again, if I was ministering to another, I would remind them that God is still in control even when He isn't answering as they want. When we pray for someone and instead they choose to live life their own way, apart from God's best for them, we can still know with certainty that God loves them and that only love will win them back. Good can still come from what seems most hopeless. I'm proof of that in many ways. Some of the worst choices I've made in life have ultimately made me into the woman I am today. Shouldn't I believe God will make good come of this situation, too?

I once again lean on history to prop me up in my despair today, and I lean on truth as revealed in Scripture.

> *"And we know that all things work together for good to those who love God, to those who are the called according to His purpose."* (Romans 8:28)

I keep fact checking the verse above, specifically the phrase "the called" as it is written in my version of God's Word. Other versions I've used just say "called," and to us that sounds better rolling from our lips. I have to believe the word *the* is there for a reason or else it wouldn't have been added to this particular translation. I don't know the Spirit's intention for anyone else, but He is using this for me today as my reminder that the issues that I'm facing, the ones that are so crippling for me, are meant for me. I am *the* called one for this trial for His purpose. Maybe I am called to this season in order to grow me. Or maybe my account of what I'm dealing with may minister to some who will read this section on living out of control. Maybe it's for you.

It could be used for those reasons and many more that may never come to mind. I just know that God is sovereign, and whatever He allows into my life can be used for my good and His glory.

You know how people tell you that God will never give you more than you can handle? Yeah, that's not a thing. It's not a verse, and it's sure not the way God operates. He gives you things all the time that you can't handle or bear up under so that you will turn to Him and allow Him to be your burden bearer.

Just so you know, the verse people are misquoting is about God not allowing us to be tempted beyond what we can bear without providing a way out. That's 1 Corinthians 10:13. Look it up.

In my situation I don't want to be the person who has to bear this. Fact is, I am the weak person whose lap this has landed in.

Thankfully, I have a strong Savior, One I can be honest with and cast every care upon.

Personalize this. Know that God will never allow into your life anything that He doesn't intend to work together for good to you, *the called,* according to His purpose.

Believe

Believe that God has a plan, even when it isn't evident. If you have studied Scripture at all, you have found a long and patient plan of redemption unfold over the history of humanity after the fall of Adam and Eve. God always had a plan to restore the relationship between Himself and mankind.

I'm a pretty simple-minded girl and honestly don't get what took so long. Why allow the story to unfold over time? Why not just send Jesus the day after the fall? I have no clue what the answer is. I just know God is God and I am not. There's a reason for that: I'm not qualified for His role in the universe. That's one admission that keeps me real before Him. Even when I don't understand, even when there seems to be a simpler way for things to work out, He is still God and still in control.

Because I believe that as it applies to the larger sense of how the world operates, I have to embrace that concept in my own little world as well: When I pray for something God says no to, I am forced to take a step back from the emotion of that no and try to see things from His perspective. Maybe a no will allow Him to work mightily in me or someone else. It is possible that a yes to me will hinder what He wants to do in others.

I have to consider the fact that my viewpoint is skewed by my desire for ease. I want things to work out the easy way so that I don't have to deal with pain or disruption in life. Isn't that normal? If you take a look at your own prayers, isn't that the underlying goal? When we pray for God to remove an obstacle, isn't our motive that we don't want to take the long way around? We want a straight line to our goal with no hindrance. We forget that the journey to our destination is where God does some of His greatest work. He strengthens feeble legs along the way. He deepens shallow faith and grows the babe into maturity.

When I pray for another, my real fear is that their pain and hardship will cause me pain. Isn't that especially true for parents? We pray for and hope for ease for our children. If they have a smooth ride, then so do we as the ones who love them most.

No parent enjoys this next train of thought: What if our prayers were instead focused on our children's ultimate best and not their ease? If their spiritual growth requires hardship, are we willing to pray for that? Would you dare to pray "whatever it takes" for your children if you know that may mean a disruption in their lives and pain in yours?

Many years ago now, I prayed "whatever it takes" for my oldest son, Adam. Then I quickly added, "Anything but jail." Within weeks of that prayer, Adam had his first jail visit. I say first since there were several more to follow, including one actual prison term. There's no way to express the pain of that season or the fear that came with knowing my son was in the midst of such evil and wickedness. Prison is an unimaginable place for us law-abiding citizens, and the reality of what happens there is indescribable. Riots and bullying aren't on TV solely for dramatic effect. They are real. Prison is a horrific place, one my son never wants to enter again. That season made an impact on a young man who was charting his course with one bad decision after another. Now, as a dad and family man, Adam would be the first to tell you that prison changed his life. That prayer of a mother willing to ask God to do whatever it would take was one that God used to allow the worst to happen in order that good might come of it.

On a side note: I released my first book, *Unmending the Veil,* while Adam was incarcerated. Would it amuse you to know that he had gang-bangers lined up to read a Christian novel when he was finished reading it? One of his cell mates planned to have a verse from Job that I had used in the book tattooed on himself: "Though He slay me, yet will I trust Him" (Job 13:15). That same young man was a former Satanist who had an upside-down cross tattooed on him. God can do mighty things with our pain.

Consider that verse from Job. Circumstances come, and we feel God is slaying us. I had a conversation about this with Him not so long ago. My conclusion was this: He can only live through me once I'm slain. An alive Lisa fights for control and remains unwilling to allow the Spirit complete control over her life. So yes, I believe He is slaying me. I will trust Him.

When I feel too wounded to even pray, for myself or others, I repeat these three things to Jesus:

I know that You love me.

I believe You have a plan.

I will wait to see how it unfolds.

When nothing makes sense, when all you can do is be still, be real, and believe, these three truths will remind you: You are loved, God is in control, and time will allow you to see His goodness, even amidst the chaos.

OUT OF CONTROL:
TAKEAWAY

LOOK WITHIN:

List areas where you try to control others and outcomes:

_____

_____

Do you have a Lord issue? Are you willing to call Him Savior but not Lord over your circumstance?

_____

_____

Describe a time when you fell from the mountaintop to the valley.

_____

_____

Do you have trouble being still when God prompts you? Give an example of when you were still and when you acted. What were the outcomes?

_____

_____

From the first word that spoke our world into existence, God has been sovereign and in control. No matter the rising flood waters you may be facing in life, you can trust Jesus to reign supreme over the situation. He sits as King forever.

KEY POINTS:

-   Control is merely an illusion.

-   God has a plan even when He seems to be absent from your desperate situation.

-   Our greater issue is not control, it is our refusal to allow Jesus to be Lord over the situation.

PRACTICE THE DANCE:

How can you apply the Key Points of this section to your day-to-day life?

_____

_____

_____

LEARN THE LYRICS:

-   If you didn't at the beginning of the topic, read Psalm 29.

Do you notice a common phrase at the beginning of many lines of this passage?

_____

A theme I notice in my version is the phrase "The voice of the LORD..." It's repeated multiple times to call our attention to the fact that the LORD speaks, and His voice is the final word. This encourages us to seek out what God says in His Word on every matter. Our topic today points us toward the sovereignty of God. If you struggle with trusting God's control over areas of your life, try this activity:

Do an internet search using a phrase like this: "verses on God's sovereignty." You will get dozens of results and lists to view. Take your journal and write out verses that most resonate with you. Next, spend a few days looking up those verses and reading the adjacent verses for context. In this way, you will find a few verses that you can claim for this season. Make index cards and keep them with your Bible and journal. Every time you are tempted to try and take control over difficult areas of your life, use your claimed verses as your reminder that God can be trusted to do His job. Your job is to allow Him to be the Lord over your life.

- Write Romans 8:28 in the space below.

_____

_____

_____

Over the next week, begin your journal heading with this verse. Each day, note one way in which you have seen good come from what seemed to be a bad situation. Remember, good can mean many things. Good can come in the form of your growth, your deepening faith, or your obedience in the most difficult situation.

SOUND OF THE MUSIC:

Your history with God creates a familiar tune for you to dance to, even when you don't know the steps. Reflect on how He came through in a situation that seemed hopeless.

_____

_____

_____

_____

NEXT STEPS:

One way to live your life in light of this topic of control is to take an honest appraisal of the areas where you try to control others and outcomes. You will only make progress once you know where you tend to take over.

- Learn to be still when prompted.

- Be prepared to act in obedience when you know God is leading you.

- Allow Him to lead you no matter what your feelings tell you.

STRIKES A CHORD:

What have you learned through this topic that requires further reflection?

_____

_____

_____

SING YOUR OWN SONG:

Whether you pray silently, aloud, or write your prayers in your journal, be real with the Lord as you pray. Express areas of doubt and ask that He show you examples of His activity in your life. Ask for reminders of His past faithfulness to strengthen your faith today. Begin with this opening:

"Your Word tells me that nothing will be impossible with You. I look around at my life and circumstances and these areas seem impossible…"

LIVE UNDER CONTROL

"The Fruit of the Spirit... is self-control."
(Galatians 5:22-23)

The premise of this entire book is that when you know you are loved, you are free to live your life under new management in every area. To live under the control of the Spirit of God is one of the most difficult tasks for many of us. We step out on the dance floor and pretend to know the steps but then stumble along and never really get the groove. That's me when it comes to certain areas of self-control.

I'll begin here, a place where I have already admitted I struggle: my mouth. Taming the tongue has been a constant struggle my entire life. I have vague memories of second grade and how I rarely got to play at recess because I had to stand and face a brick wall as punishment for talking too much in class. If you knew me, you would just nod and say, "Yeah, not surprised."

The older I've gotten, the more my voice has changed. Rather than talking just to talk, I now talk to help. Sure, that's good when I'm speaking to a group of ladies who want to hear me talk, but what about this family of mine when I want to "help"? I have all these handy suggestions that I want to share. That's helpful, right? I mean, I've been there and done that: had kids, struggled as a young parent, traversed the job market, etc. Why shouldn't I give my two cents? Why would anyone not want me to?

It's funny that this topic came to mind just yesterday. The more I considered it, the more I knew it would be a chapter someday. I happened to be making the eight-hour drive to see my oldest son and his family in South Carolina as I pondered what I would include. Now, here I sit at 5:30 the next morning, in my hotel bed, typing about last night's failure. So much for someday.

I was one of "those mothers," the one who comes to town full of suggestions and criticism. I even heard myself as I was speaking and finally gained some control over my mouth. My son is dealing with an unforeseen job loss and move. They are having to start over, and they are struggling to get back up on their feet. I want so much more for him than the hand he's been dealt. It seems as if he takes one step forward and two steps back. It pains me, like, it literally causes pain in my heart to watch his struggle. As a parent of an adult child, I am limited. I can't take over, which is in my nature. I can't make him think like me, which I try to make him do. So in the absence of any control over the situation, my mouth engages.

When we love someone and want what's best for them, it's only natural to try and help God with the work He's doing in their lives. That's exactly what I do. I lay in bed last night thinking over some of the things I had said and how frustrated I was over the entire situation. I knew I wouldn't sleep. Trouble sleeping is typical for me while traveling, but because I hurt over my son and his family's situation, I was even more burdened than usual. A phrase came to mind: live out of control, the chapter title of what I had just written.

That one thought began to ease my tension. I have no control over what happens now or next. God does, though. He is in control. With that truth in mind, I went right to sleep and slept well. Funny how living loved can bring peace even in the midst of watching those you love suffer and struggle and fight to survive.

I prayed early this morning, sitting with God the Father. After pouring out my heart, I feel He spoke these words to me: "Tame your tongue, be helpful, love them, and go home." What wise advice from an expert in parenting. I can now see how these four guidelines are required in every area of living under control of the Holy Spirit.

Tame the Tongue

*"She opens her mouth with wisdom, and on her tongue
is the law of kindness."* (Proverbs 31:26)

Yeah, I've pulled out the Proverbs 31 woman for this one. I needed to look at her this morning as I prepare for the day ahead. Notice, she opens her mouth with wisdom. The truth is, much of the advice I'm giving my son is wise, based on my own lessons learned by life experience. There is nothing wrong with sharing wisdom, but the second part of the verse above sets the tone. What does it look like to share wisdom with the law of kindness on our tongue?

For me it's in the delivery of what and how I say things. I'm straight-forward in the way I speak. Ask anyone who wishes they hadn't asked my opinion. The older I get the better I'm am at controlling my mouth, but still, I know I can be too direct. While it all stems from the desire to be helpful and guide others in the right way, I know I can come off as pushy. Recently, I've watched a few TV shows and movies where the mother or mother-in-law is pushy and opinionated. Every time I see that, I think how much I don't want to be that person. Truth is, I'm that person without the Spirit's control and the law of kindness governing my tongue.

Sometimes taming the tongue isn't just in our delivery, it's holding our tongue and not giving advice even when we think we might burst if we don't. Besides our children, this lesson applies when we deal with aging parents, co-workers, spouses, and friends. I mentioned before about interfering with God's work. When we are too often the source of wisdom for others, we get in the way of them going to the true Source of wisdom. In our attempts to advise and guide, we may be inadvertently keeping the person we care about from seeking God through prayer and Scripture reading on their own. Why would they if we keep stepping in and solving their problems?

When we think of taming the tongue, we think of not being rude in line at the store when we've had to wait too long. That's an elementary lesson of the faith walk. The true test of keeping your tongue under control is how you use it to speak into the lives of others and how you balance when to speak and when to bite your tongue.

Another angle from which to view this:

"He who rebukes a man will find more favor afterward than he who flatters with the tongue." (Proverbs 28:23)

Other times taming the tongue implies that we must speak hard words. If you are a non-confrontational type of woman, then speaking up when it's needed is just as hard for you as not speaking up is for me. Though I do speak too easily at times, I can also be guilty of not advising wisely when I should. Sometimes I'm just too tired for confrontation. We all get there. It's easier to allow something wrong to slide than it is to address it.

Since we always keep Jesus as our model, then we allow His activity to guide our own. Much of His interaction with the religious leaders of the day was confrontational, so much so that they ordered His death. I'm not saying that we are in such a precarious position, but we are called to speak truth when the truth is needed for the good of someone placed in our sphere of influence, even when we know they will push back.

We began this chapter with the words: "The fruit of the Spirit is…self-control." I know in my case that my self can't be trusted to a great degree, but my self and my tongue under the Spirit's leadership can be controlled and used wisely.

Be Helpful

"Do not withhold good from those to whom it is due, when it is in the power of your hand to do so."
(Proverbs 3:27)

We are called to be helpful, even when it doesn't align with our own personal agenda. That often requires the power of the Spirit to guide us, not just to motivate us to get outside of ourselves and help, but also to direct us where and how much to help. Need abounds no matter where we look. There's a homelessness crisis in our nation, at risk children and youth, hunger and poverty. The need is so great and overwhelming, it's easier to shut down and do nothing than to figure out where you can and should help.

Where is your place? There are the big-picture needs, like those of orphans worldwide and helping ministries and missionaries. Your help in those areas should be governed by the Spirit's leading. What breaks your heart? Whose plight so consumes you that you absolutely have to volunteer or give money to their cause? That's helping in a broad sense.

In a narrower sense, the best place to start is in your today. What needs of others are you aware of today? Who and what has God brought into your path, and how can you help?

Today, we will rent a truck and move my son's furniture. I can lend a helping hand and be encouraging. I can help with the baby while they move, but I don't have to take over as is my usual way of operating. I can allow them to make the decisions and simply nod and go along with it. As adults, they need to make their own way without my "expertise" in every area. This will be a struggle for me, since I'm a take-charge personality by nature. My son is too, so you see the head-butting that could take place. A Proverbs 31 woman would allow her grown son the freedom to take charge today and allow him room to grow and thrive.

There is a delicate balance between being helpful and being a hindrance. I'm not sure I will ever strike the right balance in this area, especially where my kids are concerned. When I see someone I love in need, I want to help. Our verse from Proverbs 3 may help to shape our way of considering the extent of our help.

Let's begin with the second part of our anchor verse for this section: "when it is in the power of your hand to do so." There are obvious times when we do have the power to help others, so we help.

In light of the delicate balance between help and hindrance, should we always help?

"Do not withhold good from those to whom it is due..." Today is the first time I've really dissected this verse and absorbed the qualifier, "to whom it is due." Normally, in Christian culture, we are made to feel guilty if we don't help everybody all the time. Maybe that's why we stop helping altogether. How can we possibly keep up with everybody all the time? This verse may help us when helping others.

I don't think the word *due* necessarily means worthy of our help. I think it might be pointing toward the idea of timing. At that time are they due your help? Or, at that time would your help interfere with the work God is doing in creating their dependence on Him and not you and others? Again with the delicate balance concept. Your only way of knowing if the person is due is through your own dependence on God through the Spirit's leading.

Love Them

For this we will revisit the Proverbs 31 woman. I've read these verses with fresh eyes this morning and now see it from a new perspective. Though we often consider her a woman who seems to be working herself to death, the real undercurrent of this passage is love, a woman who exemplifies love in action.

When we are loved by a God whose actions are evident in our own lives, we, too, can love in action. When what we do doesn't line up with our verbal expression of love, then how can it be called love? Love acts.

It requires the power that only the Spirit can give to love people well. At times, loving well means allowing life and consequences to happen to the one you're tempted to bail out. Tough love is great in theory until you comprehend just how tough tough love is while watching your child or friend reap what they've sown.

Since those of us with a rebellious and independent streak tend to learn best from life experiences, including mistakes, consequence can be the best teacher. It helps to mature those still trying to do things their own way. You will find moments in your life when love requires your inaction. Weak legs won't get any stronger if you keep carrying the one who keeps falling.

What if it isn't a case of needing tough love? What if it's a case of having powerless love?

In the Book of Acts (3:1-10), Peter and John were walking into the Temple when they encountered a lame man begging at the Temple gate. When he asked them for help in the form of a handout, they stopped and told him look at them. That they would have to instruct him to do so causes me to speculate that the man was looking down or away in what was likely shame over his predicament, even though we later read that the man had done nothing to cause his situation. He had been born lame and had no means of income other than depending on the generosity of passersby. Or maybe he had been stepped over and over-looked so many times that he didn't expect someone to stop.

Whatever the case, verse 5 tells us that the man gave them his attention expecting to receive something from them.

"Then Peter said, 'Silver and gold I do not have, but what I do have I give you: In the name of Jesus Christ of Nazareth, rise up and walk.' " (Acts 3:6)

These two disciples were wise enough to know they didn't have the power to change this man's life for the better, but they knew the name of the One who did. Here's a point we shouldn't miss: At times people need our help, but even when we are willing to help, we are powerless. There are occasions when only the activity of God can stand a person on their feet.

My son is trying, yet he has consequences that have followed him from years of bad decision making. I can keep giving him money – I'm technically able to – but it isn't always wise or what's best for him. He has to stand. He needs to see God's hand in his life and not only mine. The balance that I spoke of earlier will always be something I must pray over. In many ways I'm not able to help and am left with a heart filled with powerless love. I can't provide him with a stable job or the will to walk out his life following Jesus. I can only resort to trusting in the power of Jesus to make his life more stable.

I know I'm not alone in this. You face learning a similar balance of loving well. It's a common issue, one that God uses to grow us and show us His activity in our lives and in the life of the one we're tempted to help beyond the point of what's wise. Ultimately, because we know God loves us, we can believe He will guide us to know how to love best and not easiest. Easy is always saying yes to the one you love. Best love sometimes says no.

Go Home

I have the cutest, sweetest little grandbaby in the history of the world. I'm sure of it. To leave her and go home was difficult for more reasons than just me being in love with her. Because of my son's current situation, Ellie isn't living in a stable environment. Until they find a new place to live, she is in upheaval. I wanted to fix that. Now that I'm back home, I still want to fix it. I can't. This is my son's journey with his family and his journey with Jesus.

What I can do is remember Who is in control. If you recall, that one point is what helped me to go to sleep that first night in my hotel – and every night after. I'm not leaving my precious family out on their own. Instead, I'm leaving them in the capable hands of the God who loves them all more than I ever could.

A thought came to mind while I was there and fretting over the issues my son is facing. God carried me through my toughest times to the life I now know. He will do the same for Adam. It was because He carried me that I was able to draw near to Him. My lack of interference in Adam's situation will allow God to be God to Adam.

I can't stress enough how difficult it is to resume normal life here while knowing Adam is facing such difficulty. It takes intentionality to let go of all the things I would change about their situation. Here is where my faith is most tested, and I have to choose: I can pray for

Adam and allow this to all play out, or I can butt in and make sure things are handled the way I think they should be.

In case you're wondering, so far, I'm praying. I said before that love is action. In this instance my action is prayer. That's enough. That's everything for a worried mom.

Living under control isn't only about behaviors or self-will. It is listening to the Spirit even when the answer is contrary to what your heart is telling you to do. I made a point in an earlier chapter that the heart lies. Any activity that stands in the way of God's progress in your life or another's is a lie.

You and I will face these dilemmas for our entire visit on this earth. We can't help it when we love flawed people. Just remember, difficulties here aren't forever. They are mere seconds in light of eternity. Someday Adam will get it together. Someday I will quit stepping in. In the meantime we must all learn to live under the control of a Father to whom we can entrust the ones we love.

LIVE UNDER CONTROL TAKEAWAY

LOOK WITHIN:

Do you have issues with taming your tongue? If yes, give examples of when that's most difficult for you.

_____

_____

How do you personally love in action?

_____

_____

Do you struggle with saying no, even when you know your help might actually be a hindrance? Give an example of when you helped anyway and the outcome.

_____

_____

_____

Think of a time when you were powerless to help. How did you make it through that season?

_____

_____

_____

_____

KEY POINTS:

- Tame the tongue – speak when you should and don't when you shouldn't.

- Love them – love is action, but action doesn't always mean help.

- Be helpful – recognize the balance between help and hindrance.

- Go home – allow God to be God.

PRACTICE THE DANCE:

How can you apply the Key Points of this section to your day-to-day life?

_____

_____

_____

_____

LEARN THE LYRICS:

- Read Proverbs 31:10-31.

Married or not, we can all learn from this woman's life. Don't use this list to beat yourself up over areas in which you're not excelling. Focus instead on areas where you are making strides. In what areas do you see growth? Give examples.

_____

_____

_____

What areas need improvement, and what are you prepared to commit to in order to achieve positive changes?

_____

_____

-    Write verse 26 in the space below:

_____

_____

_____

In order to offer wisdom to others, wisdom must be attained through a close walk with Jesus and reading His Word. Being intellectual isn't wisdom. Having street smarts isn't wisdom. Wisdom is having God's mind on a matter. That can only happen by the renewing of your mind.

Proverbs is called the Book of Wisdom. Over the next few months, read one chapter each day along with your other reading. You will often find days when what you read that morning will give you wisdom to make decisions and to speak into someone else's life.

The second part of verse 26 mentions the kindness of our tone. Where do you fall in this area? Are you kind in your help toward others, or is your default to criticize?

_____

NEXT STEPS:

It's time to take inventory of yourself and your love in action. Are you helpful or a crutch for the cripple? Consider areas where you continually step in and refuse to allow someone you love to land when they fall. It could be something as seemingly insignificant as bailing out a child who didn't complete their homework or as big as giving money to the one who needs to feel the sting of burning through their own.

Consider how changing this behavior might reshape your interactions with others. This requires major self-reflection. Journal your thoughts.

STRIKES A CHORD:

What have you learned through this topic that requires further reflection?

_____

_____

_____

SING YOUR OWN SONG:

"Plans are established by counsel; by wise counsel wage war." (Proverbs 20:18)

To live under the control of God goes against the grain of what we feel and requires waging the war of our lives. Seek wise counsel through prayer. Write out your prayer here:

_____

_____

_____

Use your journal to work through the Key Points of this topic. Record the counsel you receive through God's Word and through His Spirit.

LIVE IN SAFETY

I can't help but hear the quirky tune of "Safety Dance" in my head. Even if you're not a fan of '80s music, you may know the song. The lyrics make little sense, but the song says "you can dance if you want to." Since I began to work on this topic, the tune has followed me around and reminded me that I can dance in safety while loved by the Father.

You don't have to fear dark shadows lurking behind every corner. Love allows us, as believers, to face each day knowing that God upholds us.

> *"Fear not, for I am with you; be not dismayed, for I am*
> *your God. I will strengthen you, yes, I will help you,*
> *I will uphold you with my My righteous right hand."*
> (Isaiah 41:10)

Since I find the above verse written in Holy Scripture, I know it's true. Yet there are times when I fear, and I can actually feel the oppression by the enemy crushing and disabling me.
Scripture also warns:

> *"Be sober, be vigilant; because your adversary the devil*
> *walks about like a roaring lion, seeking whom he may*
> *devour. Resist him, steadfast in the faith, knowing that*
> *the same sufferings are experienced by your brotherhood*
> *in the world."* (1 Peter 5:8-9)

The enemy is real, so anyone who underestimates him risks falling for his schemes. His intention isn't simply to hinder; his objective is to destroy us as believers. Since he can't steal our salvation, he settles on damaging our walk, crushing our spirit, and causing us to doubt.

I recently went through a dark season where opposition got the best of me for a while. At the time, I wasn't sure what was happening. I just knew something was dreadfully wrong. When it was over and the sun reappeared, I sat one morning and asked God what had happened. A conclusive answer never came. Beyond the fact that the experience has allowed me to write this chapter from an up-close and personal perspective, I don't think I will ever fully understand.

When no answer came, I did the next best thing: I asked how to prevent it from happening again. From there, during my quiet time and through Bible reading, the Lord outlined some safety principles for me to follow. I have to believe they will benefit anyone who reads this since we are all susceptible to the wiles of the devil. I know there are many more principles than what I'm offering here, ones unique to you, but these will get you started. Remember, when facing a tough season of your own, ask questions through prayer. God will give you your own warning signs to watch for.

Safety in Numbers

We need the many. To think any of us can remain an island unto ourselves and maintain spiritual health is dangerous and opens us up to the enemy's attack. If you consider the real-life application of a safari, you will see the comparison of how we are safer in fellowship with others.

On a safari the group is instructed to remain together. When in transit, for example, if a lion sees the group in a vehicle, he sees them as a whole, not as individual members. To that lion the collective group is a bigger-than-him foe, so he will not attack. Let the group stop and one member wander away, and the lion won't hesitate to pounce.

Spiritually, it's the same with us. When we are attached to the body of believers, we are formidable foes. Alone, we are an attack and fall waiting to happen.

When viewing the past through the lens of safety in numbers, I realized during my season of assault I had allowed myself to become isolated. My husband and I are attending a new church, so I feel disconnected. I'm not yet surrounded by people I know as my church family. I know it will take time for bonds to form and to feel at home there, so in the meantime I must make sure to surround myself with other believers in the form of family and friends.

We need the few. I've been privileged to experience this firsthand. First, through the intercessory prayer of two Godly women who, during a season of spiritual, mental, and emotional weakness, held me up until I was strong enough to walk again, just as Aaron and Hur did for Moses (Exodus 17:8-16). And second, through two friends and co-laborers in the faith who help keep me on track in the midst of this overwhelming book project. Their continued encouragement has enabled me to keep going when I am tempted to give up. God used them to drive this point home.

Recently, I had fooled myself into believing that no one believed in what I was doing with this book, specifically the two friends and co-laborers I mentioned who are working with me as I write. Through a misplaced email, an unanswered text, and my own doubts, I assumed I had lost their support. That wasn't the case with either, but that was the flaming dart the enemy shot toward me. In my unsuspecting and alone season, that arrow landed and spread like wildfire, allowing natural self-doubt to consume me and render me paralyzed for some time.

We believers sincerely need others. If you are anything like me and tend to withdraw into your own little world, then this warning is for you: The enemy waits and watches for an opportunity to catch you wandering from your safari group. He will pounce the moment he's given the chance. I can't encourage you enough to keep strong believers in your corner to walk with you on this journey through life.

I kind of roll my eyes at myself now, as it seems pretty ridiculous that a comedy of communication errors could so easily cripple me. There was more to the story, however. Besides me being isolated, I had fallen for something that is a recurring issue for me: I cast more than a quick peek toward tomorrow.

Safety in the Present

Speculating over the future is nothing new for me. Every self-respecting control freak does it. We have to in order to know what's coming so we can get a handle on how to manipulate it. Does that sound familiar? Sure, we look toward tomorrow pretending to be wise, but it's less about planning with wisdom and more about us ensuring the outcome that we desire.

The future is a dangerous place. Over the years I have found that a prolonged visit will only disable, disillusion, and disappoint me. (More on these topics in the chapter Live in Today's Light.) Why I keep allowing my mind to future-gaze, I'm not sure. For many believers, though, that's a recurring theme, looking ahead toward a future we can't alter at the expense of our sanity today.

Another misstep that led to my oppressive season was allowing my dream for the future to become an expectation. I took my own vision and credited God with giving it. When I found that my project wasn't going to work out the way I expected, I became disillusioned and was soon derailed. I thought a particular direction had been God-given, but it wasn't. My misunderstanding Him in such a colossal way snowballed and had me wondering if I had ever heard Him at all. Crazy how mishearing one thing can give the enemy enough ammunition to do the wide-spread damage he did to my confidence.

Now that I've experienced the fall-out from my misguided expectations, I've learned a valuable lesson: In my daily work life, I try to accomplish that which is in front of me without regard for what will become of it or the direction it will take. Rather than considering the outcome of what I write, I have to trust that when I write anything at all, God will use it for His purposes, big or small. If I am surrendered to Him, isn't it His decision to use or not use me?

On a personal level I have to learn to do the same thing. Each day I try to make the most of the day given me. That applies to me as a wife, mom, and daughter. All of those titles invite me to worry about the future for my husband, kids, and parents. To consider the distant future in any of those areas will only usher in disabling fear, disillusionment, and disappointment.

You have a similar obligation to glance toward the future in order to make tentative plans, but only a quick peek is safe. There are holidays, vacations, and retirements to plan, deciding which schools your children will attend or what you will major in at school. Since our future is often crafted by our choices today, it makes sense to consider the future with some forethought. Just don't allow forethought to become an extended stay. What's the point of trying to figure out the elusive tomorrow when you're only promised today?

Today is a guarantee. Live in it. Thrive in it. Make an impact here in the now. For me personally, if I can do that, then by the end of each day I feel a sense of success that brings peace. Each today blazes a trail toward your future and sculpts what it will look like. If you really want the future of your dreams, it all begins with living in the safety of the present.

Safety in God's Word

Through carelessness of my own, I lost sight of the importance of safety in numbers and safety in the present. However, the one place I knew I was safe during my time of confusion was my daily dwelling in Scripture. While abounding in doubts over my call and abilities, I trusted God's inspired Word.

Sometime during those weeks when I faced such obvious opposition, I was led to Matthew 4. What landed me there was the desire to hear the words of Jesus Himself. Because I couldn't rely on my feelings or what I thought I was hearing internally, I sought out red letter words, ones I knew could be trusted. When you arrive in the New Testament, Jesus' wilderness experience is the second set of red letter words you encounter, the first being the record of His baptism.

The moment I began to read the wilderness account, my first thought was how accurately it described what I was experiencing in my own life. To label it a valley season didn't feel accurate. I wasn't exactly in a low place; I was in a barren place. In hindsight, I now look at it as a season of oppression rather than what I had considered opposition at the time. Opposition is an opposing force, to be expected from the enemy. Oppression actually takes you hostage and renders you ineffective. The fact was: opposition became oppression because I allowed it. I didn't fight back with truth. The enemy deceived, and I ate.

I'm not saying I was led by the Spirit to some kind of wilderness temptation season like Jesus, but I will admit I accidentally dragged myself there through my own carelessness and overzealousness.

No matter how I ended up there, my best means of enduring it was to view Jesus' account and model that. WWJD, right?

"It is written..." (Matthew 4:4)

Those were the first words Jesus spoke each time when confronted with the devil's temptations. Jesus knew His best defense was the written Word of God. It's our best defense as well.

Don't miss the underlying point. Jesus knew Scripture and was able to combat every temptation thrown at Him by the enemy. Yes, He was God – the Word made flesh (John 1:14) – but as Man, He had studied Scripture and internalized every truth. Only knowing the truth will protect you from the enemy's lies.

My journey through these verses was what gave me the most hope, along with the realization that God had a plan to use my difficult days to reach others. While scanning through commentaries on Jesus' wilderness experience, one suggested that His temptation season was allowed and approved by the Spirit of God so that Jesus would officially solidify his commitment to His calling.

I want to believe that is so for my own purposes, that the season of doubt strengthened my commitment to what I know I am called to do. I may never fully understand why it happened, but I don't have to. I just have to trust Him to use every moment of my uncertainty for His glory. If it was solely to share this truth with you, my reader, then it was all worth it.

Safety in God's Plan

God loves me. I never doubt that. Love is still love when discipline factors into the way He deals with me. We so often think a difficult or testing season shows God's disapproval. However, I believe there are times His approval is what leads us to the wilderness. In Jesus' life, His season of temptation came immediately after His baptism and God saying, "This is My beloved Son, in whom I am well pleased" (Matthew 3:17).

When you face tough seasons, don't make assumptions based on what you are feeling. The testing of your faith is God's handiwork in crafting His vessels for His purpose.

"My brethren, count it all joy when you fall into various trials, knowing that the testing of your faith produces patience. But let patience have its perfect work, that you may be perfect and complete, lacking nothing."
(James 1:2-4)

In my own journey through the wilderness, the key word that led me was patience, or lack thereof. Notice in the verse above the role patience plays in making us complete. If we compare this to the wilderness verses in Matthew 4, we will find the third of Jesus' temptations was based on patience. When the enemy offered to give Jesus all the kingdoms of the world, he was offering Jesus a short cut, the impatient way out. Jesus didn't fall prey to the temptation but instead replied with another "it is written" statement. Patience was having its perfect work in the perfect Man.

That thought resonated with me. In the time prior to my season of oppression, I had wanted God's plan for me to be fulfilled in my time and way and not His. When my expectations were broken, I was hurt and frustrated.

The fact was, and still is: God's timing and plan are perfect. When, and only when, we are ready (complete and lacking nothing) will He bring about His best plan for us in a particular situation. I have to believe if we continually hinder the growth process with our own little bouts of pouting, like I did, we will never be ready. Since I believe that, I have to change my approach and allow patience to have its perfect work in me as the verse says. I can help the maturing process by learning from this season and agreeing with God that His time is indeed perfect.

You can do the same. Allow Him to have His way in you, even if what you're waiting for still hasn't arrived. Rather than crying, "Now!" be ready to accept His, "Wait," all the while knowing His timing is perfect.

Safety in God's Presence

Because of my many safety violations, my once steadfast trust in the Lord plummeted. I was afraid to listen for His leading since I feared getting it wrong again. Without realizing what I was doing, I took my eyes off the presence of God, an action on my part that completed the perfect storm in which I panicked and sank.

Peter's example in Matthew 14:22-33 comes to mind. Before I make the comparison, I will say that I admire Peter for getting out of the boat to begin with. Just like Peter, I thought I had stepped out in faith and believed I was taking the right steps. My intentions were good and my faith strong. Trouble was, I was stepping out on a word of my own.

One day, a secular song by a Christian band played in the background of a show I was watching, and somehow that rattled my spirit enough to wake me up to the truth. I was in panic mode in most areas of my life because I couldn't see Jesus. He hadn't moved; I had. There was a barrier I had created because of disillusionment and doubt. It was like I was shouting over a wall when I prayed. The warmth and intimacy I've known with Him for so many years felt cool and distant. I was within touching distance, yet separated by a wall I didn't even know I had erected.

It was all me. I had gone into protection mode and wouldn't allow myself to hope or hear. Since I had fabricated my own future plan, when that plan went awry I was afraid to trust anymore. I was more afraid of trusting me than Him. It was never that I thought God had failed me. I was disgusted with myself and my own imagination and feared I had missed Him in other ways.

More detrimental than disconnecting from the body and my encouragers, I had withdrawn from the One I am created to abide in. That was the key factor in why I was feeling such an emotional and mental mess. That one realization after making the connection with the song unlocked the door in that wall I had erected. I walked through and things were almost immediately back on track.

Soon after that day, a moment happened with my editor. I tried to explain what had happened and how I was so crippled because I had gone the wrong way. The way she simplified my conundrum made me feel pretty silly. She said, "So you misheard and went down the wrong path. So what? We all do that. Just back up and go down another path."

Her words were simple and her advice wise. We all get ahead of God's plan at times. It can be our excitement or impatience that causes it. Whatever the case, we can't allow it to hinder our willingness to try again. Instead, we can trust that He will use the times we mishear or misunderstand to grow us or use us, as in the creation of this lesson on learning to safety dance.

I couldn't have written these principles from my usual place of trust and intimacy. Any insight I gave would have been a faraway memory from my past. Instead, I needed this recent season of butting my head against the wall of my own making to give me fresh revelation and perspective.

The idea of the perfect storm comes to mind again. All of these principles I've addressed here are vital individually. Even a small fail in any area can wreak havoc in your spiritual life. My great error was that I let my guard down and every area was affected. The enemy had a field day with my emotions because I let him in. That wall I unknowingly erected between myself and my Protector placed me on the outside of our safari camp. Of course the lion pounced; that's what lions do.

In all areas you must guard yourself, but no area compares to being vigilant in maintaining your nearness to Jesus. Abiding in Him is the only place of true safety you will ever know on this leg of your eternal journey. There will never be a time when the enemy doesn't prowl like a lion waiting to catch you alone and with your defenses down. The roaring lion may be the king of the jungle, but Jesus is the King of Kings and has power over the enemy. Your nearness to Him is your protection. Remember:

*"Fear not, for I am with you; be not dismayed, for I am
your God. I will strengthen you, yes, I will help you,
I will uphold you with my My righteous right hand."*
(Isaiah 41:10)

God upholds you with His righteous right hand. You need to be diligent in staying put. Any moment distance or isolation is felt, you need to begin asking questions. If your spiritual life and quiet time feel stagnant, it may be a sign that you have placed distance between yourself and Jesus. It may be out of fear, hurt, or even unrecognized rebellion. Whatever the cause, the only remedy is to move back in. Open an honest dialogue through prayer. Admit that you can't see Him or feel His intimate presence. I started there, with that simple admission. Healing came nearly a split second after that conversation. It can for you too if you feel at all displaced from the presence of God. All you have to do is lean in to the next-to-you Jesus. He hasn't moved.

LIVE IN SAFETY:
TAKEAWAY

LOOK WITHIN:

Recall a season when your own carelessness led you to a wilderness situation or season.

_____

_____

Of the safety principles, which do you most need to focus on as an area of growth: Safety in Numbers, the Present, God's Word, or His Presence?

_____

_____

We often try to help God work out the details of our future. List ways in which your own plans have collided with God's. What short cuts have you been tempted to take?

_____

_____

_____

What was required to undo your mess?

_____

_____

KEY POINTS:

- To underestimate the enemy is to invite his attack. Don't venture away from the body.

- A long look at the future can disable, disillusion, and disappoint.

- Internalizing God's Word is your safety net and ammunition.

- God's timing and plan can be trusted.

- Be vigilant in maintaining your nearness to Jesus.

PRACTICE THE DANCE:

How can you apply the Key Points of this section to your day-to-day life?

_____

_____

_____

LEARN THE LYRICS:

The Many:

- Look up Hebrews 10:25.

You will find that this collective group has the purpose of encouraging one another. How have you found and given encouragement through your local church?

_____

_____

The Few:

-   Read Proverbs 27:17 and Ecclesiastes 4:9-12.

Both passages give good reason to maintain an inner circle. Who would you consider your inner circle?

_____

_____

If you don't have them already, utilize both verses to set you on a course to find those few on whom you might depend. Pray that God would send you the perfect few for your specific season.
The One:

-   In John 15:1-8, Jesus uses imagery of the vine and branches to express the critical nature of our relationship with Him.

Take the next few weeks, visit and revisit this verse. Make a list of truths you find there as you dissect His statements one at a time. Use your journal to track this passage verse by verse. The Spirit is your Teacher. Trust that He will illuminate new truths to your spirit and open up your understanding as you read.

NEXT STEPS:

If you are prone to fear the future, research scriptures related to fear and build your arsenal of "it is written" verses. Make index cards or create a special "I will not fear" page in your journal. When the enemy fires darts of doubt, you will be able to hush his taunts with God's truth.
Develop your own safety principles. Beyond what I've offered, look at your own history. What can get you off track? Narrow in on activities, attitudes, or actions that cause you to fear or doubt. Record your findings.

_____

_____

_____

STRIKES A CHORD:

What have you learned through this topic that requires further reflection?

_____

_____

_____

SING YOUR OWN SONG:
First, read Psalm 91 and from there, craft your own prayer of protection to the Most High.

_____

_____

_____

Abide this day under the shadow of the Almighty, knowing He will be with you through every tomorrow. This is such a power-packed scripture that you may find yourself returning to Psalm 91 season after season.

LIVE IN TODAY'S LIGHT

"Your word is a lamp to my feet and a light to my path."
(Psalm 119:105)

The love song God sings over His Bride is intended to illuminate the dance of life. Rather than stepping into His arms and gliding through our day, many of us are still too tangled in yesterday's dance to get the footing for today. Or some, like me, are so busy gazing toward tomorrow that we stay tripped up, unable to learn today's steps. I'm personally working on the dance of today and invite you to join me.

I suppose we all toggle back and forth between yesterday, today, and tomorrow in healthy and unhealthy ways. Yesterday has its benefits, and so does tomorrow, but today is your only promise. In the pages to come, we will peer into the advantages and pitfalls of time travel. Hopefully, by the end of the chapter, we will all agree that living in today's light is where our dancing feet belong.

TODAY:

"Give us this day our daily bread." (Matthew 6:11)

In the Lord's model prayer, the phrase above carries with it wisdom that goes far beyond our physical body's need for food. It speaks to our spirit's need for provision for the day. We need both physical and emotional strength to face the complicated and often chaotic days of this life. God offers all that we need for each day and every "now" moment. The verse below is one I keep posted on my refrigerator:

"...[A]s your days, so shall your strength be."
(Deuteronomy 33:25)

When my step-dad passed a few years ago, the hospital chaplain came to speak to my mother. Her wise advice has stuck with me since. She said regarding prayer, "Don't ask what's next; ask what now?"

Isn't what's next more often our question? Why is it so difficult for the human mind to remain trained on the day? In my case it's control-based, me wanting to have some say over what happens next – as if I'm capable of or qualified for that.

We must learn to live in the day and in the now. Because it requires concerted effort on my part to keep myself focused on today, I begin many mornings asking "What now?" as a reminder to remain in the light of today.

"The LORD is my shepherd; I shall not want. He makes me to lie down in green pastures; He leads me beside the still waters. He restores my soul; He leads me in the paths of righteousness for His name's sake." (Psalm 23:1-3)

The verse above is a beautiful picture of walking with God in the present. Notice the present-day terminology. David doesn't say, the Lord was my Shepherd or will be my Shepherd. David says the Lord *is* my Shepherd. The action words are present tense: the Lord makes, leads, and restores.

Get to know your Shepherd of today and His moment-by-moment leading. With your mind set on today, you are free from worry and open to all He wants to show you of who He is and how much He loves you.

Yesterday has lost its grip and tomorrow has no cause for concern for the one who's dancing with Jesus today.

135

YESTERDAY:

> *"Do not remember the former things, nor consider the things of old. Behold, I will do a new thing, now it shall spring forth; shall you not know it?"* (Isaiah 43:18-19)

If you could hear the Disney tune playing in my head, you would sing along with me, "Let it go. Let it go."

Paul says,

> *"Brethren, I do not count myself to have apprehended; but one thing I do, forgetting those things which are behind and reaching forward to those things which are ahead."* (Philippians 3:13)

I'm with Paul. Forgetting those things which are behind is a true blessing for someone with a past like mine. You may be able to relate and not want to consider past failures. Or, you may love to look back at your glory days and revel in your proud accomplishments. Either way, the past can be a hindrance to your today, just as looking too far ahead can cause you to stumble.

Don't get me wrong; I'm not hating on yesterday. Yesterday is a teacher we can trust. It also holds memories of first kisses, weddings, and rocking babies. A happy childhood filled with good memories is a gift from God. When you can look back with fondness at your past and come back to today with gladness, rejoice. There's nothing wrong with a little time-hop here and there.

Problems arise when our visit to the past becomes a stay-cation. I have been and I know people who are past-dwellers, people who live in the dimly lit shadows of time gone by. Some of the most profound healing I've known with the Wonderful Counselor was experienced by visiting my past and tracing the roots of some of my present-day weeds to old wounds. I still do it on occasion in a healthy and productive way.

I have shared already how at first I wouldn't ask God the Father for much. I traced the root of that behavior back to my reluctance to ask my earthly dad for things. I guess I didn't want to be a bother to my dad and carried that same feeling into my walk with God. It was a good thing to remember that from the past and allow it to open my eyes in the present.

Every weed of today has its roots in yesterday, even if it's not a far-off yesterday. To illustrate: During a hectic season when many demands are pulling us in different directions, we may eventually find ourselves angry at every small interruption in life. Something insignificant can happen and we react in an unfitting-for-the-situation way. The one little thing that might cause us to blow wasn't the issue. It was the many little things over the course of days, weeks, or months that compounded until a weed sprouted and we react rather than respond. We all have those seasons and can recognize how a building up of yesterday's stress can affect our today.

I encourage you to visit yesterday in pursuit of healing from today's weeds, just don't pull up a chair and stay for too long. A look back is intended to assist you today.

A good example of looking back with safety is recorded in Joshua 4. The Israelites were told to set up memorial stones after God parted the Jordan River for them to cross.

*"Then he spoke to the children of Israel, saying:
'When your children ask their fathers in time to come,
saying 'What are these stones?' then you shall let your
children know..."* (Joshua 4:21-22)

A look back can:

- Remind you of times when you noticed God's activity. I actually have my own collection of Stones of Remembrance that I keep as a reminder. Each has a small picture painted on it to remind me of some significant moment in my walk with God. Remember the story of how God took the taste for alcohol away from me? I have a stone with a little skunk painted on it that a lady gave me after I shared that story at an event.

- Help in your emotional healing process as you trace your own weeds back to past hurts.

- Teach you the hazards you need to avoid in your present.

What the past isn't designed for is defining who you are. Every day you are a new creation in Christ (2 Corinthians 5:17). The years I spent looking back, agreeing with the adversary that I was still that woman, were stolen and unproductive years. When you're convinced you are who you were, you can't possibly be who God has made you to be.

To look back at God's goodness is therapeutic and gives you hope when you're facing the worst odds. Jesus is the same yesterday, today, and forever (Hebrews 13:8), so yes, remember His deliverance in times past as a way to be reassured of His deliverance today.

TOMORROW:

As promised, I will pick up where I left off in Live in Safety. Remember that I mentioned how an extended visit to the future will only disable, disillusion, and disappoint, and how I tend to look toward the future at the expense of my sanity today? Let's take into consideration how dwelling on the future can negatively impact our today.

Disable

> *"Therefore do not worry about tomorrow,*
> *for tomorrow will worry about its own things.*
> *Sufficient for the day is its own trouble."*
> (Matthew 6:34)

Contemplating all that the future may hold can lead to disabling fear. Even the most faith-filled Christian tends to struggle with fears over money, health issues, and the future for our children. There are just too many things that can go wrong.

The Bible addresses the topic of "do not fear" more than 365 times, so we can see it's an issue close to the heart of a Father who knows our propensity to fear the unknown.

Fear isn't my default normally, but I come from a long line of fear-filled women, so you can believe I know what it looks like. My mother and grandmother were two of the most anxious people I have ever known. I say were because my grandmother has passed from this world and fear has lost its death grip on my mother. Death grip isn't an exaggeration as even my mother will tell you. Her fear of impending events once had her so bound that she lost many todays while worrying about all the tomorrows. Her healing came through the work of the Holy Spirit as she began to walk closer with Jesus after her husband passed.

If fear over tomorrow has you in its death grip, you have one place to run…to Jesus.

"Come to Me, all you who labor and are heavy laden, and I will give you rest. Take my yoke upon you and learn from Me, for I am gentle and lowly in heart, and you will find rest for your souls. For My yoke is easy and My burden is light." (Matthew 11:28-30)

This is a familiar verse, one in which Jesus calls you to come to Him, not only for salvation, but also for daily reassurance that He is still God, and He is still in control. Jesus will take from you the burden of fear and offer you rest in return.

Disillusion

Every generation says something similar: "Back in my day, things were so much simpler, so much better." My parents say it.

I tell my kids that. To see the deterioration of the world, how our culture's moral landscape is so different now, we can only become disillusioned when looking at the nation we will someday hand over to our children. It's easy to lose hope.

Political and social arguments are growing louder and more heated all the time. You can't read your social media feed without noticing the escalation. For a natural hermit like me, that only makes me want to close myself off from the world even more. No matter how much we try to buffer ourselves from it all, we can't help but see that things are only getting worse.

All I can do about the future of this nation and world is to try my best to focus on my present. I know my call is to help lead others closer to Jesus. If I can do that, then I've affected the future of those I reach and the ones who surround the one walking nearer to Jesus. It's the same with you. If you are walking out your call in this life, then you are positively affecting the future of all those in your path.

"But seek first the kingdom of God and His righteousness..." (Matthew 6:33)

This verse is our reminder that we must seek a deeper spiritual life, one that doesn't settle for the ordinary. That can only be done by living in the present. A deeper spiritual life will produce fruit that will impact the lives of others. Where the future disillusions, the present enlightens. That's where you will find light for your own journey, in your present day. If you are truly concerned about the future of our world, then train your attention back on what you are called to do today.

Disappoint

"Do not boast about tomorrow, for you do not know what a day may bring forth." (Proverbs 27:1)

I recently took a long look toward the future and tried to determine how God might make things work out on a particular matter. I began envisioning how I wanted it to turn out and allowed my mind to run wild. Speculation became expectation. Next thing I knew, I believed my own version and was disappointed when my way wasn't God's way. To be completely honest, I was more than disappointed; I was devastated and felt let down by God. But how could I be let down when God hadn't set up those unmet expectations in the first place?

Unmet expectations can wreak havoc on our faith. The older I get the more I realize the danger of having expectations at all. Maybe it's the writer in me, but I sure can create a world in which my expectations eclipse reality. When I live in the present day, only then are my expectations kept realistic. A mind focused on today doesn't have time to forecast a future.

I'm not suggesting a negative outlook, but I am proposing that we manage expectations and ensure they are based on our only sound point of reference: God, through His Word.

"Eye has not seen, nor ear heard, nor have entered into the heart of man the things which God has prepared for those who love Him." (1 Corinthians 2:9)

The one thing you can expect with certainty is that the Father who loves you has better-than-you-can-imagine things prepared. They just may not look like what you ask for or expect.

To look ahead and try to determine what's to come is too heavy a burden for any of us. God spoke into my spirit recently saying, "I carry the future. You just carry today." I knew what He meant. He still technically carries today, but I do carry my cross of today. I have responsibilities and demands on my time. For a planner like me, narrowing down my concerns to one day at a time is freeing.

Doesn't that set you free as well, knowing you only have to make it through today?

Tomorrow is a darkened doorway, one that will only be illuminated once the door opens. Stop trying to jiggle the doorknob in order to enter a place you don't yet belong.

For us future-dwellers, how can we effectively keep our mind trained on today?

I have begun a new exercise each morning. I scope out my day, what I hope to accomplish, and then set no further expectations than that. Outcomes will be what they are. When I don't get something done due to life's normal interruptions, I try not to allow it to affect me and simply put it on the list for tomorrow.

I'm fifty years old and just realizing that what I've always considered to be interruptions to my day aren't interruptions. To be pulled from what I have planned to help others is the business of doing life. I used to get so frustrated over a last-minute phone call where someone needed me to drop what I was doing and run to their aid. Okay, I can still get frustrated, but at least now I understand that is part of living and loving others.

Jesus wasn't kidding when he said, "Sufficient for the day is its own trouble" (Matthew 6:34).

Each day requires my all, so why spend today's energy on tomorrow when I know tomorrow will make its own demands?

Another good mental exercise is to focus on three feet around me, no more than that. On a recent episode of a TV show about Navy Seals, a character told of when he was training to rock climb and how he became paralyzed by fear. His instructor told him to just focus on three feet above him, climb that, and then tackle the next three feet.

I took that to heart. Now I look at today, quickly scan the week or maybe the month to come (my next three feet) to allow for tentative planning, then train my eyes back on today.

Earlier I admitted to feeling let down by God, but even at the time I knew God wasn't to blame. Maybe to say I was let down by my faith in what I thought would happen would be more accurate. For several weeks I took quite the tumble spiritually. I wasn't someone I even recognized.

Normally, I feel like Joshua, ready to engage the enemy in order to take possession of the Promised Land. When Joshua returned from the land of Canaan with the other spies, he believed the enemy was surmountable. Not the others who went with him, though. They considered themselves grasshoppers in comparison and gave a bad report (Numbers 13).

I became the other spies for a season, complaining and fearful and unwilling to take additional steps in faith. Every obstacle in my path felt monumental, while I felt like a wee-little grasshopper.

I kept wondering where that bold and willing-to-take-risks woman had gone. Normally I'm prepared to rattle the gates of hell. What had happened? The enemy fed me a bushel full of lies, and I ate. He towered over me, telling me that I was insignificant and had nothing to offer. He mocked all I have accomplished and assured me I was on a crash course with failure.

It was more than the enemy's assault that kept me trembling in a corner, binging on Netflix rather than writing. The reason I lost sight of me was that I had lost sight of Jesus. He is who I am now. In Him I live and move and have my being (Acts 17:28). So because I couldn't see Him, I couldn't see the me He had been raising up this past decade.

Spiritually, I wasn't boldly approaching the throne any longer. I was mumbling faraway prayers in doubt. When I understood that, I took that one step back toward Him and all the doubts began to fade. I accepted the fact that I had allowed my visit to the future to trip me up.

I see a trend emerging: Have you noticed how many recent spiritual valleys I keep writing about? The process of writing this book seems to keep me tossed around with highs and lows. After my many personal stories that seem to litter chapter after chapter, I see the hand of God crafting in-the-moment experiences for me to write from an up-close perspective. I'm not standing on a faraway hill looking at a valley that I visited years ago. I've been trudging along through the valley as I'm writing.

Maybe through some of my stories you see yourself and your own struggles as you learn each dance. I know for me it's much easier to relate to the in-process dancer next to me rather than the one who seems to be perfected and know all the steps. So here I am, flailing around on the dance floor next to you, making you feel right at home. You're welcome.

The concept of an internal, spiritual work comes to mind. What if God is using this book to grow me by making me sit down and write out what I've experienced and what I've learned? Am I willing to obey and keep writing if this only reaches me?

That possibility would normally bring deep disillusionment after all the time I've invested in this project, but not now, not in light of how God has framed this in my mind.

That God would spend a year and a half with such intention to deepen my faith and remind me how He has loved me with true intimacy is the sweetest thought to have surfaced in my mind in ages. Now that's love! If He thinks I'm worth this much time and effort, then I can only love Him more for His relentless love and pursuit of my whole heart.

Since you're reading this as a completed book, you can believe that He has purpose for these words to reach you. Somewhere, amidst the pages, He has something for you to learn or remember. He considers you worth His time and effort. Not just effort reflected in this book, but in His relentless love and pursuit of your whole heart all along.

With skillful precision He crafts our lives in such a way that we are reshaped into the likeness of His Son, just as a potter does with a handful of clay (Jeremiah 18). Be the clay in the Potter's hands. Allow Him to complete His work within you. Walk with Him in the present and through the trials of your current circumstances and know He has a purpose for all that you endure. Trust what He is calling you to do today even when the outcome seems pointless. God's redeeming work within you is worth the best efforts of you both. And who knows, maybe the work you and I accomplish in each of our todays will touch the life of another in such a way that they will see that They. Are. Loved.

LIVE IN TODAY'S LIGHT
TAKEAWAY

LOOK WITHIN:

Where do you most often reside: yesterday, today, or tomorrow?

_____

What issues from yesterday linger in your present day?

_____

_____

List a few vital lessons that yesterday has taught you:

_____

_____

_____

What worries over tomorrow steal from your today?

_____

How can you view tomorrow in a healthy way without the risk of losing focus on today?

_____

_____

_____

KEY POINTS:

- Focus on what now rather than what's next.

- A look back can remind, help, and teach.

- Focusing on tomorrow can disable, disillusion, and disappoint.

PRACTICE THE DANCE:

How can you apply the Key Points of this section to your day-to-day life?

_____

_____

_____

Do you find you are disabled, disillusioned, or disappointed over future concerns? Give specifics below.

_____

_____

_____

LEARN THE LYRICS:

- Commit Psalm 23:1-3 to memory. If you know this passage in one translation, challenge yourself by learning it in at least one other translation.

- Read Exodus 16 then complete the section below: Notice in verse 3: Rather than trust God in their today, the people looked back at their past through foggy lenses. Slavery was no better, but their panic and the enemy's lies convinced them they had been better off in captivity. Freedom's worst day far surpasses captivity's best.

How does verse 5 demonstrate God's provision for a holy tomorrow?

_____

I never cease to be amazed by God and how He provides for our obedience. Since He had set the Sabbath day apart as holy, He gave the people an extra portion the day before so they would have to do no work.

What was most notable about the extra portion that the people gathered for the Sabbath (vs. 24)?

_____

_____

Make notes here of further observations from this passage as it relates to yesterday, today, and tomorrow.

_____

_____

_____

NEXT STEPS:

Going forward, what can you do differently in order to keep your mind fixed on today?

_____

_____

_____

STRIKES A CHORD:

What have you learned through this topic that requires further reflection?

_____

_____

_____

OUT OF TUNE:

If you tend to time hop, how does that affect your present reality? Do you suffer from shame or regret over your past? Are there wounds from your past that just won't heal? Or, if you often visit the future, does that cause you a sense of anxiety?

Take an inventory of the lies the enemy is feeding you in these areas. Commit to pray and allow God's truth to dispel any lies you are holding onto. Write your observations below:

_____

_____

_____

_____

SING YOUR OWN SONG:

Make the Lord's model prayer from Matthew 6:9-13 yours today. Pray this prayer in the collective as written. Then use your journal to personalize this prayer in writing.

LIVE RATTLING THE GATES

"...I will build My church, and the gates of Hades shall not prevail against it." (Matthew 16:18)

Imagine a dance so bold, so powerful that when you move your feet the gates of hell are shaken! When we each take our place on the dance floor and move to God's choreography, the gates can be rattled rather than the deceiver rattling us.

Let me begin by saying that I don't believe we are to go charge the gates in some spiritual way. What I am suggesting is that when we do what we were placed on this earth to do, the gates tremble as a result.

The concept of rattling the gates of hell has been on my mind for the past few years. While reading the encounter Peter had with Jesus, it struck me that we have the same words from Jesus to stand on. The gates of hell shall not prevail against us because we are His. The Church belongs to the King. We are indwelled by the same Spirit who raised Jesus from the dead.

Why then is the enemy better at rattling us as individuals and the Church as a whole than we are at rattling the gates? We have the power to make hell tremble. An effective believer is cause for concern in the dark world. That's why this journey you are on is crucial. For as long as you doubt and underestimate God's love, you are rendered ineffective. The enemy wants nothing more than to keep you shackled and powerless and standing as a wallflower rather than daring to dance.

Allow your understanding and belief in the love God has for you to begin to grow, and you will be closer to accepting your role as a soldier in the army of the Living God. That's what we all should be, soldiers ready to do battle every day of our lives. Instead, we are a weakened body of babes who lack the ability to fight back, much less be on the offensive.

We spend more time running away from the enemy, fearing he has some mystical power over our lives, than we do charging ahead with the battle cry of the Lord. I often hear believing women say how much the enemy is pushing them around and leaving them feeling so defeated. In a recent season I felt exactly the same. We give the enemy power over us voluntarily and without realizing it. We speak his power into our lives with our words of defeat.

In my most productive seasons, I see the enemy firing arrow after arrow. Instead of being rattled and cowering in fear, I see his attack as confirmation that I'm rockin' along in this ministry with the Lord as my shield (Psalm 28:6). If the devil ever decides to leave me alone, I have reason to worry. If I'm no threat to him, then I must be slacking.

Consider this: If you are ineffective, then the enemy will likely leave you alone. If you aren't facing assaults, then you might want to look at what you're contributing to the kingdom. I'm not saying you should be facing attacks 24/7, since I know there are times when we are so under the protection of the Father that the enemy's arrows can't strike us. I do know this, though, when I am at my most productive, going about my Father's business, the enemy will strike.

I have known less productive seasons when he came against me as well. Because my faith was so weak, he was able to keep me in a cycle of self-pity, fearing what might happen next. It felt like I was enduring attack after attack with no means of knowing victory.

Now, attacks come, but they can't keep me down for nearly as long as I used to allow. Why? What's different about me? Many things in combination have made me more of a soldier and less of a babe in the faith:

- I began to read my Bible faithfully.

- I started to apply what God's Word says to my daily life.

- I allowed the Spirit to begin the transformation process in me. I actually acted on what God said rather than acknowledging it and then sticking to my old ways.

- I pursued His love. I set out to love Him and found myself more loved than I ever imagined possible.

- I set myself apart, as much as any of us can, from the world's influence through what I watch, listen to, and who I allow to influence me.

- I began to take tiny trust-steps until I was willing to take larger ones. I always, always find Him faithful - even when things don't turn out like I expect.

I'm sure there are more contributing factors that I could share, but you get the idea. Basically, I decided that the Christian life I had been living just wasn't cutting it. I was tired of living in cycles of defeat. I knew other believers who were the real deal. I hated being a faker and finally decided to do something about it. I actually prayed a prayer for God to make me real. He did.

I don't know what it will take for you to want something more than what you now know. Aren't you tired of the enemy rattling you rather than you rattling his evil gates? That's what you'll see if you look around, fearful believers whose lives are shaken and disrupted by the enemy's temptations and distractions. That may describe you at times. I know it does me in weakened and doubt-filled seasons. To live rattling the gates is a life lived on the offense rather than remaining on the defense.

Learn to play offense!

You know the saying that goes, "Let her sleep, for when she wakes she will move mountains"? I would like something similar written next to my bed so that I see it each morning: "Let her sleep, for when she wakes she will rattle the gates."

Life on the offensive can only be lived through the certainty of God's love, knowing before every battle that the victory is already won. Nothing can ever be the same once you get even a small glimpse of God's love.

> If you consider your life ordinary, you are likely underestimating God's love for you.
> If you feel you have no purpose, you are absolutely missing the depth of His love.
> If you wonder if this is all there is to the Christian walk, then you haven't encountered the foundation-rattling love of God.
> If you know you're faking elements of your faith, then being real is just a love song away.

It's time to take your faith walk to the next level. You aren't destined to remain a babe in your faith. You are placed on the kingdom calendar for such a time as this for a reason. There is kingdom business to be about. Babes in the faith can't help much in battle, but trained soldiers can. My challenge to you is to begin to take your position in the army of the Lord more seriously. Take steps to strengthen your faith. Invest time in what and Who matters.

Stop burying your head in the sand. There is an actual battle going on the spiritual realm that crosses over into your physical circumstance. There is an enemy. You are a real target. Either train to be a soldier or keep living defeated. No matter what, you will be attacked repeatedly (John 16:33), so you might as well gear up, train, and take your stand.

This past year and a half I have experienced opposition in an unparalleled way. For brief seasons I felt crippled and made little progress, but then the Spirit would seem to lift me to my feet so that I could re-engage in the battle. God hasn't expected perfection from me, and He sure wasn't surprised when I dropped to my knees in temporary defeat at times. What He does expect and provide is a way for me to stand again.

My story isn't foreign to you. The devil comes against you from the right side and the left. This is a cross we carry as a child of God, being identified with Jesus and an enemy of the devil. We each face opposition in different ways, yet we all serve the same powerful God. We can stand.

> *"We are hard pressed on every side, yet not crushed; we are perplexed, but not in despair; persecuted, but not forsaken; struck down, but not destroyed..."*
> (2 Corinthians 4:8)

The enemy has a plan to hinder you and me and will keep hitting us with his best shots. His best shot at me came just days ago. Actually, I would call it his ultimate shot when something happened that I have long known would. I have to laugh at what must have been his disappointment at my reaction. The enemy fired, and though his arrow made contact, I haven't allowed it to hinder my mission. Peace that surpasses understanding (literally) has been mine. I recently told a friend that this level of peace makes no sense under the circumstances, yet it should make perfect sense because I walk with the Prince of Peace.

Why am I so surprised? I guess because my mode of operating in previous years was to crumble under attack. Not today. That's not who I am now. Babes crumble and cry. Soldiers fight back. We pick up our sword and stand still since the battle belongs to the Lord (2 Chronicles 20).

So now, soldier-in-training, get to work. Learn how to defend yourself. Then, learn how to attack, how to rattle the gates of the one who intends to destroy you and your marriage and your children. This is a no-joke situation you face. Be bold, mighty warrior.

Let's look at Gideon, a man God used to deliver the Israelites from the enemy's oppression as recorded in the Book of Judges. Gideon was just a normal guy like you and me. There was nothing impressive about him or his heritage, yet God knew what was in him, all the possibilities of what the New King James Version calls a man of valor. God saw who Gideon would become when Gideon only saw who he currently was.

Gideon's response when God told him He was sending Gideon to help His people is often what we feel when we're told we are to stand in battle. Gideon said:

"I am the least in my father's house." (Judges 6:15)

When I first began writing, especially when I saw how even fiction could minister to women, I felt just like Gideon. I had every excuse to not step into my role: my past, my mistakes, my sin, my lack of education. All these excuses I felt made me the "least" in the family of God. Why would God ask me to help? Just like with Gideon, God saw who I would become long before I did.

Whether you feel like a soldier or not, it's your destiny to become one. While you only see who you are, God sees who you were created to be.

"[God] calls things that are not as though they were."
(Romans 4:17 NIV)

You can train your children to be soldiers by being a soldier in front of them. Through your commitment, you can defend your marriage against the death blow of divorce that is your enemy's intention. You can't do this without faith, and faith comes from knowing God's love. Pursue love as if your life depends on it – because it does. God's love and your dependence on Him alone is the cure for your weakness in the battle.

How can you rattle the gates in your daily life? Step up and be: be the wife, mother, daughter, and servant you're designed to be. There is a version of you who lives out her purpose with intentionality and passion. Tap into her. Don't allow the world to drag you along in one fruitless pursuit after another.

"No one engaged in warfare entangles himself with the affairs of this life, that he may please him who enlisted him as a soldier." (2 Timothy 2:4)

You. Are. Loved.

Upon salvation you were enlisted and empowered. God's love equips. Now it's time to engage. A loved woman lives out that love in such a way that her life accomplishes that which it was designed to accomplish. You were designed to reflect the love of God to others. It's love that rattles the gates. You are a soldier with an arsenal founded in love.

"The weapons we fight with are not the weapons of the world." (2 Corinthians 10:4 NIV)

Love draws us into intimate prayer.
Love guides us and teaches us through the Word.
Love supplies power through the Holy Spirit within us.
Love enables us to stand and gives boldness.
Love is a Person who walks with us daily.
Love is your dwelling place.

"Now when they saw the boldness of Peter and John, and perceived that they were uneducated and untrained men, they marveled. And they realized that they had been with Jesus." (Acts 4:13)

Can the same be said of you? Have you been with Jesus? Is it noticeable in your words and deeds? The main question is: Have you received His love as real and transformational?

In the first part of the chapter, I listed some disciplines of the faith that God has used to mature me over the years. Each of these has been covered in various areas of the previous chapters, but it can't hurt to take a fresh look at them and view them as personal directives that you may want to apply to your own life.

- Set aside time to read your Bible each day.
- Apply what God's Word says to your daily life.

*"This Book of the Law shall not depart from your mouth,
but you shall meditate in it day and night, that you may
observe to do according to all that is written in it. For
then you will make your way prosperous, and then you
will have good success."* (Joshua 1:8)

The first two disciplines on the list are covered well by this one verse. Notice how the final sentence assures us that reading and applying God's Word to our lives leads to prosperity and success. Spiritual growth *is* prosperity and success. This isn't about adding dollars and cents to your bank account. It's about deepening your faith, knowing God's love in a more real and relevant way, and learning to stand as a soldier of God.

-   Allow the Spirit to begin the transformation process within you. Act on what God says rather than acknowledging it and then sticking to your old ways.

*"For if anyone is a hearer of the word and not a doer, he
is like a man observing his natural face in a mirror; for
he observes himself, goes away, and immediately forgets
what kind of man he was."* (James 1:23)

Though we could have used the Joshua verse above for this point, let's take a different approach. God's Word is often a mirror that shows us who we are deep down. On the surface is a reflection of what we want others to see, and we may even believe what they believe, but God's Word exposes us to us. When faced with me, the real me that I don't allow others to see or even acknowledge myself, I am given a choice: I can agree with God that change is necessary, or I can go on my superficial little way and keep the worst of me buried. Soon enough that flash of light dims, and I forget. My forgetfulness and unwillingness to make improvements produces little more than immature, bitter fruit. However, my willingness to change grows me.

- Pursue God's love.

"We love Him because He first loved us." (1 John 4:19)

Don't make the mistake I made of setting out to love God first. I wasted so much time thinking the burden was on me. Pursue His love for you. As you read and learn and grow, His love will settle into your belief system.

- Set yourself apart, as much as you can, from the world's influence through what you watch, listen to, and who you allow to influence you.

"Joshua told the people, 'Consecrate yourselves, for tomorrow the LORD will do amazing things among you.'" (Joshua 3:5 NIV)

The word consecrate, also translated as sanctify, means to set yourself apart as holy. We should look and act and talk differently than the world surrounding us. Like me, I'm sure there are times when you look and sound like the world. Our actions and words are driven by what we allow to shape our thoughts. Read more Bible, and you think more Bible-y (yeah, I know that's not a word). Watch tons of TV and movies, and you will walk and talk like unbelievers. Same goes for what you read and the music you listen to. Remember, Jesus isn't the only one who asks you to dance. On a daily basis, the world does too. You must choose with whom you will dance and to what tune, the world's cacophony or God's love song.

- Begin to take tiny trust-steps, then next thing you know, you will be willing to take larger ones.

"Trust in the LORD with all your heart, and lean
not on your own understanding; in all your ways
acknowledge Him, and He shall direct your paths."
(Proverbs 3:5-6)

Teach that class. Volunteer at the shelter. Share the Gospel with your neighbor. God is whispering a call for you follow Him in a way only you can hear. Deep down, you know what that is. Trust-steps are some of the most frightening of all the dance steps. We stumble and get it wrong once or twice, then give up altogether. A few stumbles don't ruin the dance. Try again to step out in faith in an area that stretches you and grows you and sometimes scares the living daylights out of you.

Can I tell you a little secret? The first time I stood up to speak at a women's conference, I peed a little. No kidding. Later I realized it was just a drop, but while I spoke, I was certain it was, like, really there and noticeable. The best part of the story is what God did as a result. (I'm so glad we're friends, so I can share the TMI stuff with you.) My entire focus was on my pants, so much so that I wasn't at all nervous. The Spirit took over and was in control of what I said. I had women come up to me afterward and tell me what my words had meant to them, so clearly it was God and not me. It's hysterical now, but that day I thought I'd die.

Moral of the story: I trusted in God and found Him faithful. After that, I knew the One who called me to speak would be there no matter what and even take over when my mind was, um, elsewhere. You can trust Him, too.

You have gates to rattle, a job to do, a battle to fight. I'm proof that God can and will do miraculous things in a life when it's surrendered to Him. The battle is His; you just need to position yourself, stand still, and see the salvation of the LORD (2 Chronicles 20).

LIVE RATTLING THE GATES
TAKEAWAY

LOOK WITHIN:

Would you say you live your life rattling the gates, or do the gates rattle you?

_____

Do you find yourself feeling powerless against the attacks of the enemy?

_____

In what areas of your life are you most often rattled: areas of service, your marriage, children, career? Give examples.

_____

_____

Do you consider yourself a soldier, a babe in the battle, or somewhere in between?

_____

What steps do you need to take to move forward and assume your position as a soldier?

_____

Do you tend to play offense or defense when it comes to matters of your faith? List examples of each.

_____

KEY POINTS:

- You are intended to rattle the gates, not the other way around.

- The enemy has no mystical power over you.

- You are destined to be a soldier, made for battle.

- God's love enables you to stand with boldness.

LEARN THE LYRICS:

- Read 2 Chronicles 20:1-30

Write verse 3 in the space below. Note what King Jehoshaphat set himself to do.

_____

_____

In response to the king's prayer, God spoke to the people through Jahaziel. We can learn from this reminder.

> *"Do not be afraid nor dismayed because of this great multitude, for the battle is not _____, but _____."* (2 Chronicles 20:15)

The prophet went on to give the people instructions. Three key actions were given to them in verse 17:

> *"_____ yourselves _____ still, and _____ the salvation of the LORD, who is with you."*

This concept of us participating in the battle with God is demonstrated by the people being told to position themselves. There is action in that directive, like reading your Bible and allowing transformation. Next, we are to take our places on the battlefield. Then we stand and watch as God fights the battle. It doesn't say stay home with your head hidden under your blankets. There's a call for us to be there and engaged. Soldiers march out to battle even when the battle belongs to the Lord.

Read verse 21 again and notice that people were appointed to sing to the Lord and praise the beauty of holiness. Write their words in the space below:

_____

_____

Some translations use the word mercy, some use love. The word translated as mercy and love means unfailing love, loyal love. The people went out to the battlefield just as the Lord had directed. On the way they sang of His unfailing and loyal love. Because they knew by experience that God loved them, they were willing to join Him in the battle even when they knew they were about to face a multitude. Verse 22 goes on to say that when they began to sing and to praise, the Lord set ambushes against their enemies. Their praise prompted God's actions on their behalf.

STRIKES A CHORD:

What can you take away from this story and apply to your own life?

_____

_____

NEXT STEPS:

Continue to apply the following concepts:

- Set aside time to read your Bible each day.

- Apply what God's Word says to your daily life.

- Allow the Spirit to transform you.

- Pursue God's love.

- Set yourself apart.

- Begin to take trust-steps.

From the list above, is there one area where you will commit to work with God over the next weeks?

_____

SING YOUR OWN SONG:

"For we have no power against this great multitude that is coming against us; nor do we know what to do, but our eyes are upon You." (2 Chronicles 20:12)

I can think of no better prayer than that of King Jehoshaphat's above. What are areas of your life that you need God's specific direction? Continue this thought in your journal and list areas where you want to begin to rattle the gates.

_____

_____

_____

KEEP LIVING THE LOVE SONG

The dance we dance with Jesus is life-long as we move to the rhythm of God's love song. We began this journey together in Part One exploring God's love and learning how essential it is to go beyond merely knowing to actually receiving and experiencing God's love in such a way that it seeps into your belief system and alters how you live out this life.

Then in Part Two we began to explore individual topics that will allow you to practice the dance. Since every believer needs to continually plumb the depths of God's vast love, there's no better way to experience His love than in daily application. Your continued journey as you work through the takeaways is what will keep your mind engaged, your eyes on the lookout, and your heart near to Jesus. Seek the God who is ever seeking you, always remembering this isn't some faraway deity you belong to. You are living life and dancing the dance with the next-to-you Jesus. He is your loving partner who wants nothing more than to be known by you.

Once you begin to live the love song, you will soon begin to sing along and share His love in the way you relate to others. You will be brimming over with the fullness of the love of God (Ephesians 3:19) so much that you'll splash a little everywhere you go. Your dance will be one of beauty and elegance. Others will want you to teach them the steps. Do that. Lead and guide others along this grace-filled dance with Jesus. They will want what you have if what you have is spectacular. Sister, what you have is already spectacular if you belong to the Father through faith in Jesus. You just need to practice the dance until love is who you are.

Discipleship

This final chapter isn't the end of Live the Love Song. It is my hope that you will keep living loved in your daily life. The topics you've read are just the beginning. I have a long list of topics yet to write, but I had to choose an ending point for this book. If you enjoyed the format of the chapters in Part Two, then I urge you to visit my site at youarelovedbook.com and download upcoming installments.

> *"Go therefore and make disciples of all the nations, baptizing them in the name of the Father and of the Son and of the Holy Spirit, teaching them to observe all things that I have commanded you; and lo, I am with you always, even to the end of the age."*
> (Matthew 28:19-20)

These are the red-letter words of Jesus. His command is for me to go and make disciples, so I take ongoing discipleship seriously. This is why I want to continue our journey together through ongoing discipleship. Upcoming topics will be released monthly on my website to allow you at least four weeks to read, ponder, and respond using the takeaway. Allow the questions and key points to lead you into deeper study by reading the entire passage surrounding the assigned verses. Commit relevant verses to memory and apply their truths to your life and circumstances. Meet with the Lord each day and let Him express His love for you through His Word, His whispers, and His presence.

> *"...that Christ may dwell in your hearts through faith; that you, being rooted and grounded in love, may be able to comprehend with all the saints what is the width and length and depth and height – to know the love of Christ which passes knowledge; that you may be filled with all the fullness of God."* (Ephesians 3:17-19)

Community

In the chapter Live in Safety, I expressed my own fall as a result of not being attached to the community of believers during a church transition. I can't stress enough the importance of being part of a local church body as well as a smaller group of believers with whom to walk out this life. We really do need each other.

In addition to your local community of believers, I would like to invite you to a Facebook Community of You. Are. Loved. readers. This will be the location where I offer additional insights, field reader questions, post topical videos, and highlight each month's topic release. Join us in our Facebook group at: You. Are. Loved. Book.

Finally, this:

BEGIN AND END EVERY DAY
WITH THIS TRUTH:
YOU. ARE. LOVED.

SHARE HIS LOVE

If you enjoyed *You. Are. Loved. Live the Love Song* and found you would like to share the material contained within, consider hosting a study group with your friends at home or at church. Since questions are provided at the end of most chapters, it will be easy to read separately and then get together for group discussion.

God may be prompting you to step out in faith and trust that He can use you to help lead others closer to Him. You don't need any special training. All you need to do is facilitate the conversation and enjoy time with other believers.

Though training isn't necessary, sometimes guidance is helpful. If you would like to host a study group and this is your first time, here are a few suggestions:

Before the first meeting:

- Allow time for books to be ordered by your study group prior to the first session.

- If you plan to ask your group to have particular chapters read in advance of your first meeting, be clear about your expectations (what material to read, highlight meaningful points, come ready to discuss) and allow them plenty of time to prepare.

- Read through the material yourself and highlight what you would like to cover. Part One chapters have fewer questions provided than Part Two, so be prepared with discussion points. Remember, if it was a concept that resonated with you, it likely will with others.

You. Are. Loved.

At the first meeting:

- Allow time at the beginning for members to get acquainted if you are inviting a broad range of people who do not know each other.

- Consider starting with an ice-breaker question and go around the group asking each person to tell their name, something about themselves, and their answer to the question.

- Open the discussion time with prayer.

- Outline expectations: read the material before coming, participate in the discussion when possible, allow all members a chance to speak.

In general:

- As you move through the material, allow plenty of time for discussion. If you have notes, make sure to include the page number so you can direct others to the section you're referring to.

- Allow extra time at the end of the meeting for still smaller group conversations, if possible. Groups of two or three are often where we find our "few," those with whom we do life and hold one another up and accountable.

GOOD NEWS

The Good News is always Jesus!

This world is a sorrowful and sinful place. Without God we are a sorrowful and sinful people, lost without Jesus.

Some say, "I'm a good person." From God's perspective, though, there is no "good enough" to merit forgiveness and salvation apart from what Jesus did when He gave His life and shed His blood on the cross as payment for your sins and mine.

The Bible describes the people of this earth as either lost or found. There is no in between. The Good Shepherd seeks the lost sheep, leaving the ninety-nine behind to find the one (Matthew 18:12). Jesus has you in sight. Jesus stands with arms open, inviting you to come.

"Come to Me, all you who labor and are heavy laden,
and I will give you rest. Take my yoke upon you and
learn from Me, for I am gentle and lowly in heart, and
you will find rest for your souls. For My yoke is easy and
My burden is light." (Matthew 11:28-30)

To come to Jesus means to say yes to His invitation of eternal life. You can never be good enough or do enough. You can only say yes.

If that's what you choose today, to enter into a relationship with Jesus and become a member of God's family, speak to Him now. Be open and honest and share your heart with Him. Your prayer may be something like this:

Dear Jesus,

I admit that I'm a sinner who needs a Savior. I believe You are the Son of God who came to this earth to die for me. Now I ask to be Yours, and I choose to follow You and confess You as my Lord all the days of my life.

If you prayed that prayer with a heart of faith, then salvation is yours today, and I call you sister. When you are saved and become His, God sends the Holy Spirit to indwell you as your Teacher and Guide. Immediately, you are a new creation in Christ (2 Corinthians 5:17). Though you are new, it takes time for the old you to fade and the world's influence to be overcome, so be patient and take time to get to know Jesus. Only He can transform you through His Word, the Bible (Romans 12:2).

Don't wander out there on your own. Find a Bible-preaching church home where you can learn and grow. We were made for community, so live connected with other believers.

CONNECT WITH LISA

Lisa is an author and speaker, a woman filled with words and a heart to share Jesus with others. Her passion is to lead women into an intimate relationship with Jesus, a desire that drives her nonfiction work as well.

Lisa's journey to her current life of faith was one filled with bumps and bruises, allowing her genuine empathy toward broken believers and the lost. With her willingness to share even her most embarrassing life moments, Lisa's stories inspire, teach, and make us laugh and cry along with her.

Connect with Lisa:
Ongoing Discipleship: youarelovedbook.com

Facebook Community: You. Are. Loved. Book
Fiction Site: lisaheatonbooks.com
Facebook: facebook.com/lisaheatonbooks/
Twitter: @LisaHeatonBooks
Instagram: @lisaheatonbooks

I would love to hear from you.
– Lisa

Made in the USA
Monee, IL
23 October 2021

79990433R00098